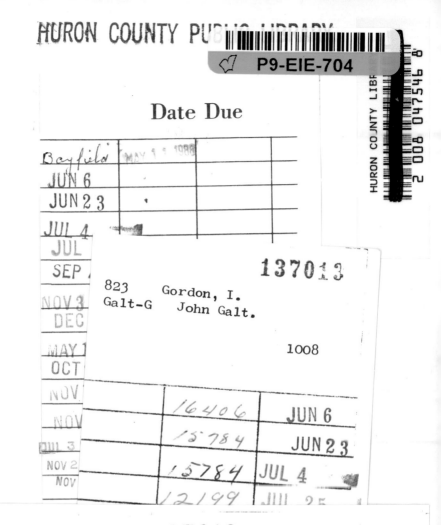

137013

823   Gordon, I.
Galt-G   John Galt.

1008

	16406	JUN 6
	15784	JUN 23
	15784	JUL 4
	12199	JUL 25

137013

823   Gordon, Ian Alistair, 1908-
Galt-G   John Galt; the life of a writer.
Toronto, University of Toronto Press,
1972.
170 p.   illus.

Bibliography: p. 157-163.

1. Galt, John, 1779-1839.

H-3027

6

JOHN GALT
The life of a writer

John Galt

JOHN GALT
The life of a writer

IAN A. GORDON

UNIVERSITY OF TORONTO PRESS

First published 1972 by
OLIVER & BOYD

First published 1972 in Canada and the United States
by University of Toronto Press
Toronto and Buffalo

© Ian A. Gordon

ISBN 0–8020–1941–2
ISBN Microfiche 0–8020–0285–4

Printed in Great Britain by
Western Printing Services Limited
Bristol

Contents

List of Illustrations

ACKNOWLEDGEMENTS

The *Frontispiece* and *Plate IV* are reproduced by kind permission of the Trustees of the Victoria and Albert Museum and the Public Archives of Canada respectively. *Plate III* is reproduced by permission of the Scottish National Portrait Gallery, whose staff provided valuable general assistance in the selection of the illustrations.

Preface

JOHN GALT the writer is a man with a double persona. He is a novelist of considerable power, with an assured niche in literary history. He also wrote, for his living, much that brought him no subsequent reputation. My major concern in this investigation of Galt's total working life as a writer has been the reassessment of Galt the novelist. One proves to be not possible without the other. Galt was capable of anything from masterpiece to competent hack-work. What he wrote at any moment depended partly on his inner drive, partly on his immediate circumstances. His success, either at the time of publication (and on occasion it was considerable) or in the hindsight of later reassessment, was curiously dependent on the luck or ill-luck he had with his publishers. The nineteenth-century publisher could make or break an author. Galt shared in both fates. Some of his best works have never faltered. They were highly regarded in his own day and today are among the near-classics. Others, of comparable quality, are buried in periodicals or in single unreprinted editions. How can a writer, who can be so excellent, be on occasion, so pedestrian? How, equally, can other works that match the quality of *The Entail* and *The Provost* and *Annals of the Parish* remain virtually unknown? The answers lie in the story of Galt's own working life as a writer and in the ebb and flow of his relationships with the publishers of his day.

This study of Galt's literary career and of his relationships with his various publishers is based strictly on sources contemporary with the events recorded — letters, diaries, wills, memoirs, memoranda, legal documents, books, periodicals and newspapers. It has inevitably at times involved some reassessment of the reliability of 'contemporary' evidence. A letter-writer is not necessarily at the time of writing in possession of the entire truth of a situation. Even Galt himself — when his memory fails — can get the 'facts' about himself wrong. My narrative does not go beyond what the evidence supports. It contains no guessing or quasi-fiction. Where I have had to be content with a reasonable inference, I have said so.

I have endeavoured to deal with all of Galt's works, and not merely his best known, the extent of my commentary on each being largely a measure of my estimate of its importance. To demonstrate the massive flow of Galt's productivity — and to establish the intellectual ambience and the time-continuum from which his novels emerged — I have attempted to pin-point all of his works not merely to the year but to the month of composition and publication. This endeavour leads to some inescapable uncertainties. Monthly lists of the time of forthcoming and published books (e.g. in *Blackwood's Magazine*) are not wholly accurate. *The English Catalogue of Books 1801–36*, though invaluable, is not infallible. Title-pages may err — two of Galt's novels, *The Omen* and *The Entail*, bear false dates on their title-pages. Publishers' announcements sometimes represent expected delivery dates, not necessarily fulfilled; and when 'the smack' bearing a cargo of books between Leith and London struck bad weather there may be a whole month's difference between publication in Edinburgh and in London. Yet for all that, it has proved possible to document from primary sources Galt's working life as a writer in some detail. Galt's other activities, though not neglected, have been deliberately documented in less depth. Galt in his time had many irons in the fire. This is a study of the working writer, a novelist of real originality, sensitive to the issues of his time.

I have many debts to acknowledge. For permission to use unpublished material in their possession, I am indebted to William Blackwood and Sons, Edinburgh, and to Oliver and Boyd, Edinburgh. For access to material and courtesies extending far beyond routine I am grateful to the officials of the National Library of Scotland; the Alexander Turnbull Library, Wellington; the British Museum; the Bodleian; The Public Record Office; the Scottish Record Office; the University Libraries of Wellington, London and Edinburgh; the Watt Library, Greenock; The High Commissioner for Canada, Wellington; the Town Council of Irvine. Professor K. J. Fielding of the University of Edinburgh generously turned over to me his working papers from the Literary Fund on Galt. Miss C. M. Gordon (Courtauld Institute)

provided documentation on Sir David Wilkie. The University of
Wellington and the Carnegie Trust for the Universities of Scotland between them provided time and grants-in-aid for travel
without which the research would not have been possible.

1. *Prologue in Princes Street*

WHEN William Blackwood, antiquarian bookseller opposite the College in Edinburgh's Old Town, shifted in 1816 to a shop in the New Town he had his eye on more than the trade prospects of this elegant district. His ambitions went far beyond selling off his admirable stock of old books and setting up as a fashionable retailer of new publications. John Murray, a Scot two years his junior and no better equipped as a bookseller, had (like Blackwood) trained for the trade in London. Now from his shop in Albemarle Street he published Lord Byron and presided over the *Quarterly Review*. Blackwood had already quietly made the move into publishing some years before; his first real success came in the year of the shift to Princes Street with the capture of Walter Scott, who agreed that Blackwood (and not Constable) should issue the first of a new series of novels, *Tales of my Landlord*. The next stage in Blackwood's progress was almost inevitable: for 50 Albemarle Street, 17 Princes Street; for Lord Byron, Scott, soon to be Sir Walter; for the *Quarterly Review*, the *Edinburgh Monthly Magazine*, which made its first appearance in April 1817. With the October issue, it became *Blackwood's Edinburgh Magazine*. Each word in the new title was chosen with care.

To begin with, he had a modest success. A monthly magazine had some advantages over a quarterly review; the novelty of the format and the dispersed interest of a series of relatively short articles had their appeal. But the manner of the early numbers was informative, uncontroversial, and not particularly lively. Fortunately, his two editors deserted him, and Blackwood had to begin again. This time, he showed his more usual skill in picking helpers, the twenty-three-year-old advocate J. G. Lockhart and the thirty-two-year-old advocate (soon to be Professor) John Wilson, who as 'Christopher North' was to remain for many years as editor in all but name. The personalities of the three men

1

established a formula that ensured the continued success of 'Maga', as the journal soon came to be known. Initially, Blackwood chose the solid core, the expositions of 'animal magnetism', the contributions on archaeology, travel, the by-ways of history, folk-lore, and literary news from London. The two younger allies saw in Maga a continued opportunity for what (for all but their smarting victims) was entertaining undergraduate satire — hence the 'Chaldee Manuscript' of October 1817 with its libellous pictures of literary Edinburgh, and the succession of onslaughts on Coleridge, Leigh Hunt, Jeffrey, Hazlitt, Keats, Shelley, and Wordsworth from 1817 to 1819. The amalgam could hardly fail. The solid core of articles was more readable than the parallel features in the *Edinburgh Review* and the *Quarterly*. The monthly musketeering was deadly. Blackwood had to pay the costs for libels; but his magazine was firmly established and could not fail to sell.

What Blackwood now sought was a novelist, who would still further diversify and enliven his magazine and expand its scope. None of the journals rivalling his included fiction. He had great hopes of Scott, whom he had so recently captured from Constable; but the future Sir Walter, friendly though he was to Blackwood and to his magazine, and prepared to procure articles, even on occasion to write one himself, knew the value of his novels. After a few printings, he firmly transferred the valuable *Tales of my Landlord* back to his original publisher, and the Great Unknown remained thereafter a prize beyond Blackwood's reach.

Had John Galt known all this, he might have made an earlier bid. When *Blackwood's Magazine* began in 1817 he was making a living writing in London where he was already a voluminous — indeed an established — author of miscellaneous books and articles. In addition, he even had ready at hand the manuscript of a novel — which Sir Walter Scott's publisher had rejected in 1813 because (two years before *Waverley*) there was no market for Scottish novels. But he was unaware of Blackwood's ambitions, and for his first appearances in Maga in 1819 and 1820 he was content to submit to Edinburgh the kind of plain journalism that made up the solid core of the magazine, a series of sober articles on the history of art and some translations from a French manuscript miscellany.

These published, and a foothold established, he submitted in March 1820 a plan for an epistolary novel, to be written in the form of a series of letters describing the visit of an Ayrshire family to London. It was an ideal form for serial publication, and Blackwood gatefully accepted, reporting that 'our friend Mr North' thought the plan 'an exceedingly good one'. *The Ayrshire Legatees* ran in the magazine from June 1820 till February 1821, and Christopher North was able to announce to readers the following year that *The Ayrshire Legatees* had 'increased our sale prodigiously'. For both Galt and the magazine it was a turning point. Galt had found an enthusiastic publisher. Blackwood had found his author.

Galt, after the magazine had printed three sections of *The Ayrshire Legatees*, was now emboldened to send to Blackwood the manuscript of his novel (*The Pastor*) which Constable had rejected. It was accepted forthwith, and when it appeared in one volume in May 1821 as *Annals of the Parish* commanded immediate sales and warm reviews. Blackwood read his London agent's report with satisfaction — 'The Annals were very popular and were selling well' — and urged his author on to further efforts in letters studded with encouraging cries — 'I am glad you are getting on' . . . 'a good and striking story' . . . 'a glorious subject' — and Galt responded with unflagging fertility. From the middle of 1820 till the end of 1822 there were few numbers of Maga that did not contain a contribution by Galt in one or other of his genres — an instalment of a story, a book review, a solid piece of writing on agricultural economics. Alongside this, he continued the themes of his two successes in a series of linked novels of eighteenth-century Scottish life, and in December 1822 Blackwood was able to advertise on the front page of a London newspaper six of these novels by Galt (three of them in their second edition, two of them in three-volume format) a total of ten volumes of novels, all published within less than three years. Scott himself could not have done more.

But Blackwood — though he was not to know it for some months — had already lost Galt. If Galt had been prepared to write on for him without demands, all might have been well, but the author required cash in hand as well as encouragement. Blackwood had not been ungenerous. He had paid well for the regular Maga contributions and had paid increasing sums for the copyright of each successive novel, culminating in five hundred guineas, between June and August 1822, for *The Entail*. This latter sum was (following Blackwood's usual practice) payable in bills at fifteen or sixteen months. By the time the bills were due, the cash-flow from sales would normally be available to meet them. If an author needed the money immediately, he could always sell the bills (at less than their face value) on the discount market. This Galt was reluctant to do. Late in 1822, when he was in Scotland completing *The Entail*, he applied to Blackwood for an advance of some £200–£300 on account of his next book, still unwritten and — as far as Blackwood understood — still unplanned. Galt had (quite justified) faith in what he called his 'fecundity'. Blackwood, however, was cautious and, reminding Galt of the bills for five hundred guineas he had just signed, refused the advance and told Galt he 'had been publishing so rapidly I would not wish him to bring out any other Book for nearly 12 months'. Galt was silent. 'Nothing farther passed betwixt us at the time, and we had no quarrel of any kind', Blackwood wrote a few months later. But the damage was done. Galt was touchy; and he needed ready money. Unbeknown to Blackwood, he made arrangements before he left Edinburgh at the end of the year to have his next novel (which he *had* planned) published by Oliver and Boyd. Blackwood had lost Galt, as he had lost Sir Walter Scott.

The final scene of this prologue was enacted in April of the following year. *The Entail* completed, Galt went back to London in late 1822 and worked solidly on his Oliver and Boyd novel. He promised Blackwood by letter a 'strong paper' for the March number of Maga; space was held for it, but finally Blackwood had to fill in with other matter. He remonstrated. Galt made excuses. By mid-March Galt arrived quietly in Edinburgh, to correct proofs for Oliver and Boyd. Blackwood was also holding proofs for him — of the second, expanded, edition of *The Ayrshire Legatees* — and Galt in asking for them was forced to disclose his presence in nearby Leith. Blackwood responded with a brief hurt note — 'you cannot spare two minutes to enquire if we are all in the land of the living'. Galt knew he had to come into the open, called on Princes Street, and told Blackwood his forthcoming novel was in other hands. 'He is still here', Blackwood wrote to his Irish correspondent Maginn, 'and comes to the shop as usual. My feelings however are quite changed though my external behaviour is not. The Prof. and Lockhart think he has behaved very ill to me and absurdly as to himself.' Two obstinate men (but, of course, they were both Scots) had differed on a matter of £200–£300. Neither, probably, knew how much each had lost.

Blackwood had lost his author. He had plenty of other writers, but none who could fill the gap left by Galt. He had the copy-rights of Galt's best novels, and the firm continued to reprint them among 'Blackwood's Standard Novels' throughout the nineteenth century. Galt, in one sense, lost everything. He con-tinued to write and publish, with unfailing 'fecundity', till his death in 1839. After a lapse of some years he and Blackwood made their peace and resumed a real friendship, and Galt re-turned to Maga and the Blackwood imprint. He had successes, and on occasion considerable sales. In the Indian summer of his final years he wrote some superb short stories. But he never matched his achievement of these three years of intense writing for Blackwood. The Galt novels of these years — the series that Galt called (and Blackwood refused to call) *Tales of the West* — stand alone, unique re-creations in novel form of a vanished society, vanishing even as Galt put pen to paper, portrayed with humour and affection but without romantic illusions. Galt had a long, and interesting, literary life. But his best sustained work was done for the bookseller in 17 Princes Street.

2. The forty year apprenticeship

JOHN GALT was born in Irvine in the Scottish county of Ayrshire on 2 May 1779. When he was ten years old his father, a substantial sea-captain (or 'ship-master') decided the time had come to share in the profitable trade that had grown up between Jamaica and the westward-looking harbours of the river Clyde. He became the owner of a West Indiaman and moved his family to the thriving Clyde port of Greenock. Galt — who in later life was to recount the stored impressions of these years in his 1833 *Autobiography* and his 1834 *Literary Life*[1] — grew up in the countryside and the small towns of the West of Scotland, a small world in itself, but a world that opened easily to the distant colonies. All this made up his unconscious education. His formal schooling — in a country and at a time when an able boy of his background had ready access to university — was quite limited. His mother on occasion was alarmed at the day-dreaming bookishness of her young son, but a succession of private tutors, a short time in the old Grammar School of Irvine, and the years from ten to sixteen at two schools in Greenock firmly directed him to the kind of education for commerce that that appealed to a sea-going merchant father. He learned enough Latin to tackle Horace; but the main bias was towards penmanship (for business); mathematics (learned, with a theodolite, under a master who taught geography and navigation to the Clyde skippers); French (for foreign travel); and English (a subject then largely peculiar to Scotland).

With this equipment, which suited young Galt admirably, he moved into the world of commerce. After a few months in the Greenock Custom House (to improve his penmanship), he went at the age of seventeen as a junior clerk with a firm of merchants in the town, Messrs James Miller and Co. He remained with the

firm till his departure for London at the age of twenty-five in
1804. Galt's memory of these active years was a happy one —
'what with business and reading, and all those sort of employ-
ments to which headlong youth is prone, I had very little leisure'.
Life had expanded pleasurably. He became a subscription member of the Public Library, which the town had set up in 1783,
and was a 'voracious reader' of English and European literature;
he began to learn Italian; he played the flute; he haunted the
theatres in Greenock and Glasgow; he went walking tours as far
afield as Loch Lomond, Edinburgh, the Borders, and south to
Durham (where he saw Mrs Siddons play Lady Macbeth); he —
staunch patriot at all times — joined a corps of volunteer 'sharp-
shooters'; with two school friends, he founded a Literary and
Debating Society. One, William Spence, was to become a mathe-
matician of note and Galt was to write his biography; the other,
James Park, became Galt's literary mentor, and the initiator of his
first book. Galt, with thirty fellow-members, entertained the new
rising poet James Hogg at the Tontine Hotel in early 1804,
leaving the future author of *Confessions of a Justified Sinner* with
a lasting memory of the literary company of the town.[2] For Galt
his small world was a lively one.

   He had already begun to write (inspired by Pope's *Iliad*) while
at school. The *Literary Life* records an ominous facility of output
from these Greenock days: a Pindaric Ode; two full-length blank
verse tragedies, one roused by Mrs Radcliffe's Gothic romances
and the other (submitted to Constable in Edinburgh and rejected)
on Mary Queen of Scots; appearances in print in the *Greenock
Advertiser*; several sets of verses printed in Constable's *Scots
Magazine*; a biographical sketch of John Wilson, which was
printed with that local poet's work in 1803; and — a long-term
task ('a work long in hand') — 'a sort of Gothic epic', *The Battle
of Largs*, sections of which were accepted by Constable for the
Scots Magazine in April 1803 and January 1804. Galt was calling as much on his penmanship as his creative ability. But he
wanted to write; and he was seeing himself in print.

   By the time he was twenty-four Galt found he had outgrown
the small world. Though he was well-regarded in his firm, he
became restless at 'the narrowness of my prospects' and determined to quit Greenock. Armed with letters of introduction to

mercantile men in London and the manuscript of his Gothic epic and just turned twenty-five, he set off south in May 1804 'with the notion that literary studies were not incompatible with business'. The letters of introduction proved a disappointment; they were no more than mere dinner tickets. Galt found himself lonely in London, writing long letters back to Park in Greenock.[3] No business opening offered, and he spent an 'idle six months' seeing the sights, reading widely especially in political science and frequenting the art galleries and the theatre. Towards the end of the year, he had his poem *The Battle of Largs* published in volume form, but suddenly struck with the fear that a Gothic epic was no great recommendation for his hoped-for 'mercantile connexions', he promptly suppressed it, though not before a few copies had gone out for review. *The Monthly Review* in February 1805 and *The Critical Review* in July gave it a chilly reception.

At last he made a start in business. He met in 1805 another young Scot named McLachan, from his own part of the country, whose business as factor and broker was returning five thousand a year. Captain Galt on this information advanced his son in excess of his patrimony ('more than *my bairn's part of gear*') and a partnership was established. It was short-lived. The firm was (unknown to Galt) encumbered before he joined it. The partners got over that difficulty, but by the end of 1807 the failure of 'a correspondent' in Greenock involved Galt in two rushed trips to Scotland to attempt to set things right. The attempt came to nothing. The partnership went bankrupt in April 1808, but secured an immediate discharge from creditors. Later in the same year 'much against my own will and opinion' he joined his brother Tom in another short-lived business venture. Galt was twenty-nine and his taste for the world of commerce was blunted by failure.

The parallel plan for literary success had gone equally slowly. In his second year in London, Spence and Park had come south 'to see the lions' and in the early summer of 1805 the three young Scots paid a visit to Oxford. There, in Christ Church, Galt conceived the idea of a life of its founder, Cardinal Wolsey. But it remained only an idea. His publications in the next few years amounted to two prose articles. An older Scot, Dr Alexander Tilloch, as a young man had left Glasgow to own and edit a newspaper, *The Star*, and a journal of applied science, the *Philosophical Magazine*. Tilloch liked his young fellow-countryman, and for the magazine Galt wrote what was more calculated than a Gothic epic to enhance the reputation of a businessman, *An Essay on Commercial Policy* (November, 1805) and a '*Statistical Account of Upper Canada*' (October 1807).

While Galt in these early London years had confined his publications to what was appropriate for his public image, in private he nourished other ambitions. He had not forgotten the small world. He had no wish to return to it, but he knew that there was in it something worthy of record. The deeper he plunged into London life, the more he came to savour the quality of the rural west of Scotland, and the literary possibilities of its language. He began on a series of rural sketches in Scots verse, though prudently made no move towards publication, and for the moment he showed them to no one. In 1805 another young Scot arrived in London, David Wilkie, from the small village of Cults in Fife, already with a local reputation for a 'Dutch' genre painting of Scottish village life, 'Pitlessie Fair'. Wilkie's first Royal Academy painting of 1806, an ironic portrayal of small-town life entitled 'The Village Politicians' was a phenomenal success and made his reputation as a genre painter of the Scottish rural scene secure. Galt, as great a haunter of studios and art galleries as he was of theatres (he was soon to write the life of the President of the Royal Academy) immediately recognized a kindred interest, and when Wilkie followed up his first London success with the homely pathos and humour of 'The Blind Fiddler' in the Academy exhibition of 1807,[4] he could contain his enthusiasm no longer.

He wrote to Wilkie on 12 May 1807, expressing his admiration, and revealing some of his own secret hopes — 'Independent of the pleasure that I enjoyed from your picture in the present exhibition, as a work of art, its truth and liveliness as a delineation of natural circumstances afforded me high gratification of another kind. Previous to leaving Scotland I often felt myself interested by the peculiarities of conduct, opinion, and notions among the peasantry, and at one time entertained the idea of describing some of them in the colloquial manner of our antient humorous ballads; but business diverting my attention here to other objects, has hitherto prevented me from accomplishing the design. I only compleated the scetch of two pieces, of which I have presumed to trouble you with copies; I do not venture however to expect that they will afford any degree of pleasure, at all comparable to the extraordinary satisfaction which I have obtained from your visible representation of a portion of the same class of ideas.'[5]

Galt retained few letters, and there is consequently no trace of Wilkie's reply, but it can hardly be accidental that in the next few years themes from the work of each regularly recur in the work of the other. One of the poems that Galt sent to Wilkie was 'The Penny Wedding',[6] the subject of one of Wilkie's best-known paintings — and of a chapter of *Annals of the Parish*. The gauche and shy young applicant in Wilkie's 'The Letter of Introduction' could serve as an illustration of Galt's first London disappointment. Later, a scene from *The Provost* will find more than an echo in Wilkie's 'The Parish Beadle'. Meantime, as early as 1807, Galt saw clearly in Wilkie's work that what one Scot could do in paint another could one day do in print.

His record of parish life lay still in the future. For the moment, Galt was more concerned to get out a solid book that would establish him in London. After the collapse of his firm in 1808, he was understandably depressed, without a settled occupation, and in a state of 'nervous indisposition' returned to the Wolsey idea of his summer trip to Oxford. He got down to the work seriously in early 1809, collected material in Jesus College, Oxford, and in the British Museum. It was his first experience of historical research, and at the cost of a 'considerable sum' he employed a young man to copy two folio volumes of original documents for his appendix. In May he was able to send Park the first draft. Park commented on it at great length. But by the time his letter arrived, Galt had laid the plan aside. Perhaps the law might provide him with the kind of career he was looking for. He entered Lincoln's Inn on 18 May. However, his 'infirmity increased'. He gave up study, and went to the Continent to recover. He was thirty, and the high hopes of success had come to nothing.

Galt was on the Continent from the middle of 1809 till September 1811. The period expanded his knowledge of the Mediterranean countries, gave him some Spanish and fluent Italian, but brought no immediate advancement either to his literary or his business career. It was a time of restless drifting —

Gibraltar, Sardinia, Sicily, Malta, the Adriatic, Greece, Asia Minor, Constantinople. He read books in the garrison library at Gibraltar and in the Jesuits' library at Palermo; at various halts he dabbled in desultory writing and translated plays; he wrote regular traveller's letters to Park in Greenock; he dreamt of big business coups, one of which included the Elgin marbles. His final months were spent on a complex scheme which, for anyone other than Galt, would have been high romantic adventure. Conceiving a plan to smuggle British goods past the Napoleonic blockade into central Europe by way of Turkey, he bought a warehouse on a Greek island, organized 100 bales of merchandise, and rode off ahead of his baggage train from Constantinople overland to the Hungarian border. The expected agent failed to turn up at the rendezvous and Galt, shedding 'tears of vexation' was finally rescued from this anti-climax by an aged Turk who took the goods (and forty-five camels) off his hands at cost. Galt duly made his way back to Constantinople, retraced by ship his Mediterranean route, arriving via Ireland back in Greenock in October 1811; unaffected, unimpressed. His health had greatly improved. The set of his mind was unaltered. He had seen the Isles of Greece, the Castle of Otranto, the Castalian Spring, the tomb of Agamemnon, the minarets of Constantinople. They all slid by, while he surveyed, took measurements, and compiled statistical tables of imports and exports for Park back in Greenock. He was John Galt, not Childe Harold.

2

Yet he had gained by the experience. The nervous, lonely, and disappointed young man who had shipped from Falmouth in 1809 returned to his home country brimming with self-confidence. He had met Lord Byron and travelled with him. He had met Governors and Archbishops and Ambassadors and Pashas and had learned to mix in a cosmopolitan society. He was still without any settled plan for his future, but in no doubt that he had one. The sense of failure was gone. He had measured himself, and was eager to get started. Early in 1811 Park had sent an edited manuscript copy of Galt's letters to Constable in Edinburgh. Constable accepted them, but later, pleading 'the difficulties of the time' refused to proceed with the publication. Park then engaged the help of the friendly Dr Tilloch, who submitted the manuscript without success to Longmans and to Cadell and Davies.[7] Galt, in his new confident mood, within a few days of landing at Greenock was back in London, interviewed — unsuccessfully — the Foreign Office concerning his commercial plans, had the manuscript of his travel letters printed at his own expense, and had arranged with Cadell and Davies to publish the book on joint account. 'Were we words instead of men', Park wrote in admiration on 15 October, 'You would certain be a verb active.'

The printing proceeded promptly under Galt's watchful eye. Dr Tilloch invited his young friend to stay with him while he was correcting the proofs, and Galt's first book was out by January 1812. Its very title-page revealed the author's preoccupations, *Voyages and Travels in the Years 1809, 1810, and 1811; containing Statistical, Commercial, and Miscellaneous Observations on Gibraltar, Sardinia, Sicily, Malta, Serigo, and Turkey*. It might be a clumsy title, but the two-volume, two guinea, work was elegant in format, in the words of the proud author 'rather handsomer than common'. *The Gentleman's Magazine* gave it a prompt and friendly three-part review extending over the February, March and June numbers and this counterbalanced the adverse notice in the May *Critical Review* and the savage onslaught in the June number of the *Quarterly*. Later reviews were warmer. The *Monthly Review* of August 1813 was friendly; the influential *Edinburgh Review* of April 1814 though it grumbled, as was its wont, about the prose style, praised Galt's 'bold and independent tone'. Apart from the *Quarterly* (which he never forgave) Galt had no reason to be displeased with the reception of his first book. He had the satisfaction of seeing it sell well, and it 'paid the expenses of my travels'.

Stimulated by this success, under the continued patronage of Dr Tilloch he threw himself into work both new and old. In January 1812 he became editor of a weekly paper, H. R. Yorke's *Political Review*. By February he had tired of this 'sedentary' weekly journalism. It did not suit his 'restless disposition' However, as a by-product of this interest in current affairs he wrote and had printed in March a 99-page pamphlet, *Cursory*

Reflections on Political and Commercial Topics as reflected by the Regent's Accession to Royal Authority. This exercise in economic journalism, which gave England much the treatment he had given the Mediterranean countries, was dedicated to Tilloch 'as an acknowledgement of Benefit and Advantage derived from his learning and friendship'. He then gathered together five dreary blank-verse tragedies he had written during periods of *longeur* on his travels and had them printed for Cadell and Davies to issue. *The Tragedies of Maddelen, Agamemnon, Lady Macbeth, Antonia and Clytemnestra* were published in May in an edition of 250 copies which, in the words of the author, 'fell stillborn from the press'. Not unexpectedly, the tragedies were badly handled by the reviews, notably *The Critical Review* (in November of the year) and later by the *Monthly Review* in March 1814 and the *Quarterly* in April 1814, and the reputation as a solid author which he had made by his *Travels* was in some danger, had he not immediately followed up this ill-advised publication with a more substantial work.

This was his life of Wolsey, long planned, and largely written in the early months of 1809. Dr Tilloch watched over his protégé in London, and Park from Greenock commented at length on the proof sheets. *The Life and Administration of Cardinal Wolsey* came out in June 1812. Galt as usual paid for the printing and Cadell and Davies handled the distribution. It was a large and impressive quarto, reflecting Galt's view of his worth. The extent of his new confidence may be gauged by his presentation copies. One went to Sir Walter Scott, who wrote him on 16 July expressing his pleasure that 'literary talent' could be combined with 'the more active pursuits of life'.[8] The British Museum copy is inscribed in Galt's hand 'To his Royal Highness The Duke of Sussex from the Author'. Galt's aspirations had expanded with his success. The life was an honest job based on documentation which, for a man who was not a professional historian, represented an impressive amount of research.

3

The life of Wolsey sold well, although the reviews were varied. But before he had time to gauge the sales or read the reviews,

Galt was off once more to the Continent and on another business venture. His self-confidence, he knew only too well, was based on a shaky financial foundation. The restless bachelor of thirty-three had run through most of his money, and the return from his writings was inadequate for his pretensions. He was paying for lavish printing and distributing copies to the nobility. Lord Byron had returned to England and made a friend of Galt: he gave him a fine quarto copy of *Childe Harold* before publication; he franked his letters; on his way to the House of Lords he 'frequently stopped' at Galt's lodging in Westminster; they dined out together. Galt was to be seen at the theatre and the opera and the art exhibitions and was moving in circles he could not keep up with. He decided to abandon Lincoln's Inn and his hopes of becoming a lawyer, sold off his carefully collected library and — as he recounts in his *Literary Life* — found himself 'penurious' but 'did not like that the world should see it' and so resorted 'to a more elevated walk of life than my circumstances seemed to justify'. Literature would have to wait, while he tried his fortunes once more in the mercantile world.

The well-established Glasgow firm of Kirkman Finlay and Co. had succeeded where Galt had failed in a considerable scheme of breaking Napoleon's embargo on the import of British goods to the Continent. Finlay, who knew of Galt's earlier scheme, during a visit to London offered him the chance of opening a branch in Gibraltar. Galt accepted, and at the end of May left for Glasgow to discuss the details. While he was in the west of Scotland he revisited 'every place I could recollect, with which in my boyhood I had been familiar'. The contrast between the 'buoyant hopes' of his boyhood and the 'circumscribed and very sober' career that seemed to lie ahead of him made it a melancholy pilgrimage. The visit to the scenes of his boyhood moved him greatly. It was to be of more importance than he knew.

The expedition to Gibraltar turned out to be another failure. Wellington's defeat of the French in Spain shortly after Galt's arrival destroyed the main reason for Kirkman Finlay's Gibraltar branch — 'I do not exaggerate my feelings,' Galt wrote in after years, 'when I say I repined at his victories'. Galt had time on his hands; he read once again in the garrison library; he improved his Spanish; he wrote 'a brief history' of the Seven Years War.

His only publications during his stay were some letters written in reply to criticism of his *Travels*: one appeared in the *Gentleman's Magazine* in July and another in the *Monthly Magazine* in August. He relapsed into a defensive gloom, not relieved when he read the review of his *Wolsey* in the September *Quarterly*, where he was described as writing 'inflated and abominable jargon'. Galt was stung by the unfairness of the review — 'every sentence of the strictures contained either a lie or libel' — and contemplated vengeance 'with a horsewhip'. When he returned to England he could not find out who had written the review, and it was a long time before 'the last ember of my resentment expired'. Later reviews were more favourable. He may well not have seen these till his return, but at least he could console himself with the long and friendly notice in the October *Gentleman's Magazine*, the respectful *Critical Review* of December and the very full coverage of the *Monthly Review* the following April. But in Gibraltar Galt could do nothing but brood, writing nothing. Even a warm letter from Scott, expressing appreciation of his *Wolsey*, lay for some months unanswered.[9] Another venture had gone wrong, and he returned ill at ease to England in the Spring of 1813, to consult a doctor.

4

The return to London acted as an immediate tonic. Congenial company and town life revived him. He took up again with Byron; and when Prince Koslovsky, whom he had met on his Mediterranean travels, arrived — and actually sought him out — Galt was delighted. They were soon 'constantly engaged', and Galt — with some pride — was able to bring Byron and the Russian nobleman together. His long-delayed reply to Scott (of 24 March) was also a letter of introduction for the Russian Prince.

Galt, indeed, was preparing to resume his elevated walk. But on 20 April he married Elizabeth Tilloch, the daughter of his patron, and the married man found that the bachelor freedom to frequent the company of wealthy and footloose Princes and Lords was at an end. Dr Tilloch made over to his daughter two of his holding of six and a half shares in *The Star*, confirming this settlement later in his will.[10] The income — irregularly paid

— was £300 a year. Pre-occupation with earning his own contribution for his new responsibilities speedily brought Galt back
to sober reality. He did a quick trip to Paris and the low countries
in May on a possible business venture but, nothing coming of it,
returned to England to make what living he could by his pen.
His friend H. R. Yorke (of the *Political Review*) was bringing an
eighteenth-century book, Dr John Campbell's *Lives of the
Admirals*, up to date. Galt contributed in 1813 the lives of Hawke,
Byron, and Rodney.

His *Travels* had sold well. Why not a sequel? Galt promptly
edited another batch of his old letters to Park, and in September
1813 there was published *Letters from the Levant; containing
views of the State of Society, Manners, Opinions and Commerce;
in Greece, and Several of the Principal Islands of the Archipelago.*
A small section of it had already been given preliminary publication by his father-in-law in the August number of the *Philosophical Magazine*. Galt, as before, arranged his own printing of
the 1000 copies. Casting around for some immediate income, he
wrote Cadell and Davies on 22 September suggesting they com-
pound for a 'fixed sum' the copyrights of *Wolsey* and of both the
old and the new volumes of *Travels*.[11] They replied the following
day, unable (owing to their 'present literary engagements') to
accept, and offered instead to publish *Letters from the Levant* 'on
the usual terms' [i.e. joint account] promising their 'best exertions
in promoting the sale of the work'.[12] The elevated walk was over.
Although the new travels were dedicated to Prince Peter Koslovsky, this was a simple cheap octavo at ten shillings and sixpence.
The ever-friendly and prompt *Gentleman's Magazine* in December congratulated 'this lively traveller' and the reviews, aided by
the best exertions of Cadell and Davies, sold the book well at its
modest price.

One further work belongs to this year. The secret ambition
Galt had disclosed to Wilkie, of writing up 'the peculiarities of
conduct, opinion, and notions among the peasantry . . . in the
colloquial manner' had been reinforced by Wilkie's successful
1812 one-man exhibition of his accumulated country village
paintings.[13] Galt felt the time was propitious to write up *his*
parish. 'In the summer of 1813'[14] — he offers no more specific
date — Galt drafted a novel entitled *The Pastor*, in the form of a

village minister's recollections in Scots prose, and submitted it to Constable in Edinburgh. 'I was informed', he recounted later in his *Literary Life*, 'that Scottish novels would not succeed (Waverley was not then published); and in consequence I threw the manuscript aside.' Wilkie's Academy picture of the previous year, the rustic comedy of 'Blind Man's Buff', was on its way to the royal collection, to be joined soon by 'The Penny Wedding'. Galt, for 'the same class of ideas', could not even find a publisher, and he had to turn to more profitable forms.

In the following year 1814 Galt was living on what he could get by writing. A new magazine was started this year by Henry Colburn, the *New Monthly Magazine*. To this Galt contributed in February (and continued in March) a satirical article *Instructions on the Art of Rising in the World* under the nom-de-plume of 'G. Haliton'. The inspiration was partly Machiavelli, whom he had just been reading, and partly his own non-elevated situation. In February (continued in April) he contributed an essay, the fruit of his gallery hauntings, *On the Principles of the Fine Arts*, parts of which had already appeared in his recent book, and it is likely that some of the anonymous contributions in the first years of the *New Monthly Magazine* are also his. He was working closely with Colburn. Having had a play (Galt would now try anything), *The Witness*, rejected by the London managers, he suggested to Colburn that a regular issue of rejected plays might sell. Colburn agreed, and established a monthly series entitled *The Rejected Theatre*. The title was not as foolish as it sounds. Colburn was cashing in on the success of the Smith brothers' *Rejected Addresses* which had run into edition after edition since its appearance two years before. When this publicity wore off, the title was altered in the third number to the more sober *The New British Theatre*. Galt was set up as editor and during 1814 and 1815 he edited, selected, wrote introductions, and contributed several of his own translated and original plays — including the rejected *The Witness*. It brought him in some income, though not without bargaining — on 27 December 1814 he wrote Colburn declaring that unless the 'N.B.T.' could afford to pay for more assistance 'I must decline the Editorship after the present month'.[15] Since he continued editor into 1815, the extra money must have been forthcoming.

By 1815 Galt, who had now one child and another on the way, knew he would have to find more regular paid employment. He sought — as his *Autobiography* says — 'nothing but an even tenor of my ways'. Rescue for a time came from the Royal Caledonian Asylum, a charity established by the Highland Society of London for the children of Scottish soldiers and sailors, in which Galt as a London Scot had been naturally interested. He was made secretary at £300 a year, and organized a fund-raising dinner, splendidly attended, the Duke of York in the chair. He wrote to Scott, suggesting he might 'provide a Song for the Dinner'.[16] When Scott pleaded other duties,[17] Galt had promptly printed a broadsheet 'Triumphal Glee by Mr Galt' which was 'sung after drinking the health of the Prince Regent'.[18] An un-published manuscript life by Miss H. Pigott[19] says that at this period he had 'his banquets graced by the Elite of the intellectual world', mentioning Lord Blessington, Edward Ellice, and J. G. Lockhart among his guests. Her account — collected from Galt in his final months of life — must not be pressed too far. Galt could have offered few private 'banquets' on his income. But he always enjoyed the company of men who mattered, and his position as secretary of an important charity gave him an entrée to London society that he did not neglect. Certainly he gave up his work for Colburn, and there are no Galt articles traceable in the year 1815.

5

He set himself, instead, to write another solid biographical work, based on his interest in the art world. Among his many London friends he counted Benjamin West, the American painter who had come to England to become the President of the Royal Academy. Galt assiduously collected West's account of his American years and in May 1816 Cadell and Davies published his *The Life and Studies of Benjamin West* as the first volume of a two-volume biography. Galt could no longer afford the danger-ous pleasure of paying printers, and he sold the copyright to Cadell for £150.[20] The book was well done and well received, requiring a second edition the following year. The *Critical Review* in June praised it, and the *Monthly Review* in November 'exhorted' Mr Galt to 'continue with every allowable degree of rapidity'. But for the moment Galt dissipated his literary energies on other plans. As a spare-time occupation he completed three cantos of a poem, *The Crusade*, and was not greatly surprised when its publication in Edinburgh (1816) aroused no enthusiasm. Seeking a more acceptable line, he threw much of his successful *Travels* into the form of a novel, *The Majolo*, which was published in two volumes in November, 1816. The hero was mediterranean, but the material of the picaresque was essentially Galt's own experiences. It sold badly. The *Critical Review* (March 1817) bluntly — and accurately — condemned it as 'scarcely a novel . . . not a piece of biography'.

This time, the lack of success was a blow. Galt had hoped for a popular success and he sadly realized that if he were to supplement his assured income by writing, self-indulgence was not enough — 'The Majolo', he wrote in his *Literary Life*, 'was the last of my publications as an amateur author; hitherto I had written only to please myself, and had published more to secure the reputation of a clever fellow than with the hope of making money; but I saw that hereafter I was destined to eke out my income with my pen'. £600 a year[21] was not enough; the pressing needs of a small family drove him to write for ready money. He appealed to his father-in-law, who introduced him to Sir Richard Phillips, an enterprising and successful publisher of elementary school text-books and of the *Monthly Magazine*. For him, Galt became — the words are his own — a 'bookseller's hack', at twelve guineas a sheet. Between 1817 and 1823 he contributed an unknown number of anonymous articles to the *Monthly Magazine* varied from time to time with a contribution to which he felt he could put his name.

The following year, 1817, produced no publications of note. Galt simply records that he wrote for 'the periodicals'. His only signed contribution to the faithful *Monthly Magazine* was a letter in July. In the same month, urged on by a Scottish lawyer of some distinction, he revised his play *The Witness* — re-titled as *The Appeal* — since there was now more than a promise it would be produced in Edinburgh. But it was not a happy year. The death of his brother Tom in 1813 had left its mark. He was still grieved at the more recent death in 1815 of his old friend William

Spence. The death of his father in August entailed a visit to Greenock and there he found his friend Park in his last illness. Galt discovered — to his horror — that a will incompetently drawn up after his brother's death had made him as the only surviving son the sole heir to his father's estate. He hastily executed a deed by which his mother was made the life rentrin, on her death Galt and his sister would inherit equally. Galt returned to London, vexed and sad, to await the birth of his third son in September; and the *Gentleman's Magazine* of November announced as 'preparing for publication' a 'Mathematical Book' by William Spence with a life by Galt. But Galt, although he had persuaded the astronomer-royal, Sir William Herschel, to provide a preface, was in no mood to complete the memoir and he laid the task aside.

Returning to London Galt surveyed his situation glumly. He was now moving freely in the London political and social world. But back at home he had a wife, and three children, and the treadmill of hack-writing. Yet, during the early months of 1818 he worked steadily with Benjamin West on the sequel to the first volume of the biography — the June *Monthly Magazine* announced that 'Mr Galt is preparing part II'. His *Wolsey* went into a second edition. His tragedy, *The Appeal*, was produced for four nights in Edinburgh with a verse prologue by Lockhart and a verse epilogue by Scott. Constable published it as a volume — at Galt's expense. Galt was becoming an established figure in the world of belles lettres.

But reputation paid no household bills, and when his Glasgow friends — shrewdly estimating his influence on the London scene — proposed yet another export venture (which involved procuring a London guarantee for shipments through Jamaica to the Spanish colonies) he promptly secured a guarantee from a firm of 'old friends', Reid, Irving & Co., and jumped at the opportunity. It meant leaving London to be nearer the centre of operations and setting up household near Glasgow. He chose Finnart, a short distance from Greenock, and there he spent the latter part of 1818. Like all Galt's mercantile ventures, it came to nothing; and Galt came to see very soon that 'the scheme would end in smoke'. But he hung on and, with time on his hands, went back to 'writing for the periodicals'. Among other work, he was invited to contribute to a newly established but short-lived journal, the *Edinburgh Monthly Review*, and for this he did an article on Nathan Drake's *Shakespeare and his Times*, which appeared in April 1819. He wrote a second romantic novel, *Birbone or The Outcast*, and submitted it hopefully to Constable in Edinburgh.[22] He had the pleasure, mixed with some annoyance, of seeing a travelling company put on his play, *The Appeal*, in Greenock. But he was bored with small-town life, pining for the activity of the south and for his London friends — 'of all my life, that residence at Finnart was the most unsatisfactory'. He was unaware, and for the remainder of his life remained unaware, that this was — for later readers if not for him — the most significant time of his life.

6

Reprieve was at hand. In Glasgow, Galt had now a solid reputation as a dependable man who knew his way around the London scene. It was not unmerited. In his *Literary Life* he noted with a touch of naive but honest snobbery that he 'was acquainted with more than twice the number of ladies of title than with mistresses of all ranks'. More to the point for his Glasgow friends, he writes that at this time he had 'upwards of sixty acquaintants, members of Parliament'. The Edinburgh and Glasgow Union Canal Company, established by Act of Parliament in 1817 to complete a canal link between the two cities, being in need of further capital had a private bill before Parliament,[23] and the Directors appointed Galt to 'superintend' the passage of the bill among his parliamentary acquaintances. For Galt the assignment was 'a Godsend' and early in 1819 he bundled his family into the Glasgow coach for London, to lobby for the Directors. The bill was lost. But the Canal Company, with justifiable faith in Galt's contacts, 'employed me again formally' for the following year. Galt recorded in his *Literary Life* with unconcealed irony his 'saponaceous' proceedings, interviewing individual members of the then unreformed House. The bill passed, and the Directors, Galt recorded with satisfaction, 'paid me for a carriage and all expenses, and handsomely'.

These negotiations were spread over 1819 and 1820. Meantime, he required an income, and his pen was working overtime.

PLATE I: High Street, Irvine, in the time of Galt

PLATE II: William Blackwood

He began by putting up a whole series of projects to Constable. He had originally offered him *Birbone or The Outcast* from Finnart on 8 December 1818 and on hearing that 'it will afford us pleasure to usher your production into the world'[24] had left the manuscript in Edinburgh on his way to London in January 1819.[25] The further correspondence of this year between author and publisher[26] shows urgent offers on the one side and on the other canny refusals. By 18 July Constable was declaring himself 'reluctant' to publish the novel — 'I should of course be willing to yeeld it to any other Publishers'.[27] Galt's offers of an edition of the Saxon Chronicle, a translation of Pausanias, and a continuation of *The Life and Studies of Benjamin West* were successively refused. Constable, for all his fair words and promises, was as little prepared to publish his new work as his older *Pastor* of 1813. Galt had to turn elsewhere for a living.

The firms of Sir Richard Phillips and John Souter were considerable publishers of elementary school text-books. Throughout 1819 and 1820, under a pair of *noms-de-plume*, Galt set himself manfully to work for them. As these *noms-de-plume* belonged to the publisher rather than the author, it is not always certain when (e.g.) 'the Rev. T. Clark' is John Galt, some other author from the publishers' stable, or even the publisher himself — for Galt in later years, when a new edition was under consideration, wished to remove 'many of the things that were put in by Sir Richard's Cooking as mere stuffing'.[20] But by considering what Galt mentioned privately in letters, what he openly acknowledged in later accounts of his life, and the unblushing re-use in some books of material Galt had already published under his own name, the following list can be ascribed to Galt with certainty. The dates are the dates of the title-pages. The actual writing belongs to the years 1819 and 1820.

All the Voyages round the World by Captain Samuel Prior, 1820 (Phillips); *The Wandering Jew* by Rev. T. Clark, 1820 (Souter) — a history and geography of the western world for 'the youthful reader'; *A Tour of Europe* by the Rev. T. Clark, 1820 (Souter) and *A Tour of Asia* by the Rev. T. Clark, 1820 (Souter) — books of travels which include an extract from *Letters from the Levant* solemnly noted as 'the production of a very intelligent and agreeable traveller', for which (were the innocent deception discovered) Galt could always plead the authority — almost — of the *Gentleman's Magazine*; *Pictures Historical and Biographical drawn from English, Scottish, and Irish History* by John Galt Esq., January, 1821 (Phillips) — a history of Britain 'for juvenile readers' of over a thousand pages; *The National Reader* by the Rev. T. Clark, 1821 (Souter) and its companion *The National Spelling Book* by the Rev. T. Clark, 1821 (Souter); *A New General School Atlas* by the Rev. T. Clark, 1822 (Souter); *The English Mother's First Catechism for her Children* by the Rev. T. Clark, 1822 (Souter) — a question-and-answer text-book mainly on natural history; and two children's books, *Gog and Magog* and *The Rocking Horse*, now only catalogue entries.

It is tempting to think lightly of such titles, written under sheer need. In fact, an examination of them — now bibliographical items of great rarity — reveals that Galt was a good writer for 'juvenile readers, for whom this Work is principally intended'.[29] He put his European travels and historical reading to excellent use and wrote, as he said in his preface to *The National Reader*, 'only well-attested facts, told with great simplicity of style', no bad recipe for a text-book. If D. H. Lawrence can be allowed some credit for a useful text-book on European History (also written under a *nom-de-plume* and in like circumstances for the money) there is no call to be condescending about Galt's activity. Galt had to live in two worlds. In public, he was the knowing man of affairs, the familiar of the ladies of title and the Members of Parliament. At home he slaved at his desk — the text-books that can with certainty be ascribed to Galt at this time run up to a tally of over three thousand pages — and he saw no reason to be ashamed of what was an honest and professional job of applied writing.

Under his own name he completed in March 1819 the delayed life, 'The late Mr William Spence'. It was published, along with a short unrelated poem, in the May issue of the *Monthly Magazine* and reappeared the following year as a Memoir in Sir John Herschel's edition of Spence's *Mathematical Essays*, 1820. The December issue of the *Monthly Magazine* had a short signed article, 'Seven Principles of Political Science. Seven Principles of the British Constitution', a by-product of Galt's now continual contact with Parliament.

For Phillips in 1819 he did a further book of a different sort, turning one of his old plays into a one-volume novel, *Glenfell or Macdonalds and Campbells*, published in February 1820. This mystery publication has hitherto only been known in a French translation of 1823, equally anonymous; and doubts might be cast on the ascription, particularly as nineteenth-century catalogues tend to assign to Galt the general authorship of anonymous Scots novels. But Galt in concluding his *Literary Life* was reminded by a friend of this old publication, and though he had not included it in the appended list of his published works, he 'instantly recollected it'. His friend wished him to include another Phillips novel, *Andrew of Padua*, but this novel 'even to the name, escaped my memory'.[30]

An apparently unique copy of *Glenfell* is now in the National Library of Scotland. Its preface calls it 'our little comedy of northern manners'. It is little wonder that Galt had forgotten it. It bears all the marks of something dashed off rapidly, a slight novelette of Edinburgh society with a farcical plot of mistaken identity and thin characters of no special merit. The only recognizable Galt touch is the appearance of a 'Colonel Rupee', a foreshadowing of the Nabob, 'Mr Rupees', in *The Last of the Lairds*. *Glenfell* and *Andrew of Padua* (if it is his) were no more than money-spinners, thrown off and forgotten, like all his work for Phillips.

In the middle of 1819 Galt turned forty. Half of his adult life was over. What had he achieved? A great deal of restless wandering, concluded by a pacific and happy marriage; three little boys; a competent income, so long as he kept on the treadmill; a series of business failures on his own account, but something of a reputation as an honourable and effective agent on behalf of others; a small inner circle of close friends, mainly London Scots; an enormous outer circle of acquaintances, many of them in the great world; thousands of pages of competent writing in pamphlets, manuals, periodicals and books, none of it likely to survive. It was less than he once would have settled for, but it was not unagreeable.

And in the meantime he continued to write, little dreaming that literary fame was just round the corner. How could he know — how could anyone know — that it was to come from a rejected manuscript he had thrown aside?

3. The years with Blackwood
I: First success

1

GALT WORKED, almost exclusively, for William Blackwood during the three years 1820 to 1822. Since the publisher retained copies of outgoing correspondence and carefully filed each of Galt's letters and notes — even a hasty scribble inviting him to share a steak — Blackwood's business-like organization enables us to follow with precision Galt's development as a novelist and the growth of the close relationship between publisher and author characteristic of the period. The Galt letters are now in the National Library of Scotland, and Blackwood's Letter-Books are still with the firm, with the strange result that the biographer today can document these crucial years more fully and with greater precision and even understanding than Galt himself was able to do, when some dozen years later, in ill health, he produced largely by dictation his *Autobiography* and his *Literary Life*. His two books remain of primary value, revealing what Galt felt in his mid-fifties; but on the details of his career they can at times be obscure, imprecise, and even in error. The Blackwood-Galt letters reveal what an older Galt had simply forgotten; perhaps, on occasion, what he preferred to forget. Largely unpublished, they are drawn on heavily in the present chapter.[1]

2

Galt began to submit articles to *Blackwood's Magazine* about August or September of 1819. His first certain appearance was in the October number with an article on the progress of the fine arts, signed 'Viator', and entitled — in line with Maga's known liking for mystery — 'Transactions of the Dilettanti Society of

27

Edinburgh'.[2] Another article in the same issue, 'The Scotchman
in London', describing visits to artists' studios, is almost certainly
his. His 'Viator' article was introduced by the Editor as 'a very
interesting paper' and Galt (8 November) expressed his pleasure
at this prefatory note and sent a 'continuation of the same', an
article on Italian painting, which appeared in December as No. II
of the 'Transactions'. Galt promptly followed up his successful
entry with an assorted batch of articles; Blackwood (23 February)
returned his paper on 'Animal Magnetism', but promised to use
the others, and the March number contained two Galt contributions, 'From the St. Priest MSS.' (a collection of historical letters
translated from a French MS. miscellany) and No. III of the
'Transactions of the Dilettanti Society of Edinburgh, on the
Progress of Architecture in England', signed — for further
mystification — not 'Viator' but 'D.B.' The April number contained No. II of his 'Selections from the St. Priest MSS.'

So far, Galt had merely found another outlet for miscellaneous
writing. But this ready acceptance by the major Scottish magazine
made him think again. He knew he was capable of something
better than competent general articles; and in March 1820 he
sent Blackwood the plan for *The Ayrshire Legatees*. Blackwood
was in no doubt. He wrote on 28 March that the plan was 'an
exceedingly good one', commissioned 'four or five pages in each
number regularly', and promised later to publish 'the whole
separately'. This was encouragement that Galt never had before,
and he responded with speed, sending in the first part of *The
Ayrshire Legatees* on 1 May; and the work ran in the magazine
from the June 1820 number until that of February 1821. The
only break was in November, when Galt did not 'feel myself in
the humour' to write an instalment.

The writing of *The Ayrshire Legatees* released Galt from the
tyranny of hack-writing. More important, it freed his imagination and his creative powers. The man who had been unmoved by
the romance of foreign travel, who had so recently been bored
with the actual life of a small Scottish town, suddenly found that
by shifting his focus, by dipping into the memories of his childhood, the small Scottish town became rich and alive. His different
return visits to the West of Scotland, the melancholic pilgrimage
of 1812, the various rushed business trips, the sad funeral journey

of 1817, and the 'unsatisfactory' residence of 1818, suddenly made sense; they had reinforced his memories and re-tuned his ear. The postscript he added to his letter to Blackwood of 1 May is significant — 'Tell our friend Mr North not to touch one of the Scotticisms'. Writing for the London papers, he had shown himself a competent journalist. Accepted by the leading Scottish periodical, he became a novelist.

The Ayrshire Legatees was structured as a series of letters written by the four main characters. The conception owes something to *Humphry Clinker*, but the letter-format had been revived only a few months earlier by Blackwood, with the publication in October 1819 of Lockhart's *Peter's Letters to His Kinsfolk*. Galt's allusion, in his instalment of October 1820, to 'our friend Dr Peter Morris of Aberystwyth' is a clear indication that he knew *Peter's Letters*. But Lockhart's book is not a novel; it is a series of descriptive commentaries on personalities in Glasgow and Edinburgh. *The Ayrshire Legatees* is a novel, simply but tightly plotted, and constructed with skill. Dr Pringle, the incumbent of 'Garnock' (near Irvine, Galt's birthplace) with his wife, son, and daughter journey to London to accept a considerable legacy. The high comedy of the raw provincials in the metropolis is recounted with innocence by the parents, with mounting sophistication by marriageable daughter and lawyer son. They are delayed long enough in the Capital for Galt to introduce them (and his readers) to the major public spectacles of 1820; and this section of the novel closes with daughter and son achieving satisfactory romances, and the triumphant return in their own carriage of the elder Pringles to Garnock.

The country cousin in London is a well-worn theme. Galt's originality in *The Ayrshire Legatees* consists in his counterpointing this with the life and characters of a small Scottish town. Every letter from the family in London is read to an assembled company in Garnock, who comment at length — in their own Scots dialect — with customary deflationary bluntness: the daughter's ecstatic letter (e.g.) announcing her forthcoming marriage is met with the downright: 'Rachel had ay a good roose of hersel'. Throughout the whole novel, Dr Pringle though at a distance keeps a close eye on his parish; and the Garnock 'plot' marches forward independently, yet skilfully interwoven with the events in London. The immediacy of impact of the letters, in their diverse 'styles' of Scots and English, and the direct transcription of a chorus of dialect voices is brilliantly carried off. It was no accident that *The Ayrshire Legatees* 'increased our sale prodigiously'.[3]

As each instalment was printed in the magazine, the characters seemed to achieve independent life. Galt (like Dickens a few years later) found himself increasingly involved with his readers, though (unlike Dickens) he could conceal himself under the magazine's policy of anonymity. But his identity was suspected in letters 'with the Greenock post-mark' and he was compelled to 'deny' his authorship. Beginning with the fifth instalment, he printed regularly a series of 'Responsive Notices to Correspondents'. It says much for his brilliant character-portrayal that at one time he had stoutly to affirm the 'real' existence of his characters (to a correspondent who assured him there was *no* Miss Mally Glencairn resident in the Kirkgate in Irvine) and at another had to fend off a correspondent who had written begging Mrs Pringle to advance part of her legacy to improve the streets in 'magistrate-enslaved' Aberdeen. Correspondents even invited the Pringles to visit *their* part of the country. Galt had found not only an enthusiastic publisher, who sent him a prompt ten guineas for each instalment. He had found, after all these years of slaving, an enthusiastic public.

Galt's first reaction to his success was remarkably ill-judged. As a canny Scot he could not bear to waste anything. He still had the 1818 manuscript of *Birbone*, which Constable had held and then rejected. Early in 1820 — before *The Ayrshire Legatees* began to appear in the magazine — he arranged to have it printed (under a new title) at his own expense in London. Blackwood's enthusiasm for *The Ayrshire Legatees*, however, gave him another idea, and on 29 May he proposed that Blackwood take over the printed sheets and publish under his imprint. After some negotiation Blackwood agreed, and on 31 July Galt formally accepted an offer of £150 for the copyright. A shipment of bound volumes was despatched to Edinburgh 'by the Smack' in October, and the novel was issued in three volumes in December, as *The Earthquake, A Tale*; *by the author of 'The Ayrshire Legateees'*. It was, like *The Majolo*, based on Galt's Mediterranean travels, picaresque, romantic, clumsily constructed. It was badly reviewed; doubts were expressed if it were, in fact, by the author of *The Ayrshire Legatees*. Blackwood loyally — and to protect his investment — printed a long review 'by a very able hand' in the January 1821 number of *Maga*. But nothing could redeem a poorly written book (Galt soon admitted to Blackwood it had been 'written rapidly') and Blackwood's final verdict (25 June 1821) was to 'wish that the whole impression had gone to the bottom of the sea'.

Fortunately it did not matter. Galt, once established with Blackwood, was bombarding him with further plans. Part of the earlier months of 1820 he had spent with Benjamin West working on the proofs of the second part of the biography. By this time, Cadell and Davies, who had published the first part, were joint-publishers with Blackwood, who thus automatically — and not unwillingly — had his imprint on yet another book by his new author, *The Life and Studies of Benjamin West, Part II*. It appeared in May and was respectfully received, even today its careful catalogue of West's paintings remaining of primary value.

Galt then turned to his second, even older, rejected manuscript, the 1813 *Pastor*. On 30 September, having done nothing on *The Ayrshire Legatees* that month, he sent Blackwood a 'portion' of the old manuscript. Blackwood rose to the bait, uttered encouragements, and Galt had the revision of the old draft virtually ready by the end of the year. On 30 November he wrote that he was planning 'my next series of communications': what would Blackwood think of an Edinburgh story? By 14 December he had completed a quite different short story entitled 'The Extinguishers'. On 30 December he 'had some thoughts of trying a sketch of a *shipmaster*'. He sent in a 'squib' on John Scott, the editor of the *London Magazine*, who was feuding with Lockhart. Blackwood continued to encourage his apparently inexhaustible discovery, and the pressure and productivity of 1820 was repeated, without signs of flagging, during the ensuing two years. Galt was sometimes working on so many things simultaneously that only a flow-diagram would chart his activity, particularly after December 1820, when he found himself with another of these agency appointments for which he had already demonstrated his skill. His new clients were a large body of dissatisfied inhabitants of

Upper Canada and their target was the Colonial Office. Canada was going to dominate Galt's life for many years. But in the last days of 1820 he did not know this, and his target was Blackwood.

3

In the next two months, January and February of 1821, Galt put the finishing touches to *The Pastor*, provided the last instalment of *The Ayrshire Legatees*, did a final set of 'Responsive Notices', offered a set of London 'caricature sketches', finished and sent in to the magazine two instalments of his 'sketch of a shipmaster', and had begun on what was to be a three-volume novel, *Sir Andrew Wylie*. For the whole of the years 1821 and 1822, Blackwood frequently had on his desk several Galt works in different states towards publication, manuscripts, 'slips' (i.e. galley proofs), printed sheets, bound volumes. It was he and not Galt who decided when they would actually be published, with the result (e.g.) that *The Pastor* appeared (as *Annals of the Parish*) out of Galt's original sequence of submission. Each of his works in these Blackwood years demands separate consideration, and this involves a decision on the order in which to treat them. They will be considered here simply in Blackwood's publication order. This, it must be borne in mind, is purely a stratagem of convenience, and the linear pattern of development thus arbitrarily imposed is to some extent a function of the method of presentation. In his years with Blackwood, Galt developed fast. But it was no simple development from book to book, for a man who could be writing portions of two or more works within a period of a few weeks.

The first in print was his 'sketch of a shipmaster', first proposed on 30 December. Blackwood (23 January 1821) asked for a 'new Series' and demanded 'sketches of London men and things'; the John Scott 'squib' he would hold over — and Scott's death shortly after in the notorious Scott-Christie-Lockhart duel suppressed it for ever. On 30 January Galt sent in the 'first of another series which I call *The Steam-Boat*'. It was set in print immediately, and Blackwood had the satisfaction of seeing in his February number the last instalment of *The Ayrshire Legatees* and the first instalment of *The Steam-Boat*. Like its companion

piece, it was anonymous, and there was no indication that both
were by the same hand. It ran in eight parts from February to
December. A late but urgently required review of Byron forced
Blackwood to hold over the April section till the next month,
and for November Galt, being busy with public affairs, provided
an article for his usual ten guineas arising from his current interest, 'The Emigrant's Voyage to Canada'. Two separate sketches
though not assigned in Maga to the *Steam-Boat* series, 'Dr. Scott's
Return from Paris' (September) and 'Mrs Ogle of Balbogle'
(October), were clearly written as part of it, and were incorporated
by Galt into the final version, when it was reprinted in volume
form.

The Steam-Boat contains, in fact, no shipmaster; he disappeared in the early planning. The central character is the hero
of the book's sub-title, 'The Voyages and Travels of Thomas
Duffle, Cloth-Merchant in the Salt-Market of Glasgow'. The
structure is episodic, consisting initially of the narrative, self-told
in West Coast Scots, of Duffle's two journeys by steam-boat from
Glasgow to Greenock. The character of the elderly Glasgow
merchant is established rapidly in the first instalment, but his real
function in this early part of the 'novel' is to be the auditor of a
group of short stories, of mixed quality, some of them very likely
salvaged from Galt's casual writing of earlier years. The book
really comes alive at the half-way point, when Duffle takes the
Leith steamer to London and attends the coronation of George IV.
From this point, Galt is on his own ground. The characters from
The Ayrshire Legatees join in, Dr and Mrs Pringle, the hussar
son-in-law Captain Sabre, with off-stage voices from Garnock.
Blackwood was so insistent that the *Steam-Boat* characters should
visit London that on 4 July he took the (for him) almost unheard-
of step of sending Galt an advance — 'to help forward the Coronation I enclose you a draft for ten guineas'.

Galt repaid the advance with interest. Duffle and the Pringles
narrate in their own idiom the wonders of the Coronation, im-
pressed by everything in the great city and yet resolutely determined that Glasgow could have done it better: the Abbey
ceremony to Dr Pringle is 'papistry'; to his wife it is 'Babylon' —
'but it was a very fine sight'; to Duffle, in his hired court-dress
with 'cockit-hat' and leg-entangling 'spurtle-sword', it compared

unfavourably with the crowning of the shoemaker king at Glasgow
— and he prints an annotated programme of the latter to prove
his point. Galt manages the London scene and the belittling yet
entranced small-town Scots with skilful irony that rises to high
comedy in Duffle's final encounter, with a countess-like street-
walker 'a most beautiful and fine lady' who turns out to be a 'wee
lass' from the Saltmarket, proof again of Glasgow's all-round
superiority.

It was all excellent periodical material. The monthly Maga
reader enjoyed Galt's 'clishmaclaver' method of switching from
scene to scene and story to story. In the revised and expanded
book form, which it achieved in July of the following year, the
defects of the desultory construction are apparent. Its best sections
continue and develop the formula of *The Ayrshire Legatees* and
add one more memorable character to the 'Garnock' gallery.

4

While *The Steam-Boat* was running in the magazine in the early
months of 1821, *The Pastor* was taking its final shape. Galt sent
it to Blackwood in 'portions' in the latter months of 1820. On
30 December, he wrote: *The Pastor* 'is all finished and I am
going over and binding him together'. Blackwood replied
(23 January) that he liked it very much 'but I fear there will be
some parts which would require a gentle pruning'. He promptly
followed up this letter with a group of 'alterations', an offer of
sixty guineas for the copyright — and a new title. Galt on
27 February accepted all three, the title gladly, the alterations
grudgingly, and the sixty guineas sadly — 'I was in hopes that
you would have given me £100'. Reading the final sheet proofs,
however, on 18 April, he confessed to Blackwood he was glad the
work was a little shortened — 'I am much satisfied with the
omissions' — and left to Blackwood the decision whether the
Annals should be dedicated to 'Henry Mackenzie Esq., author of
the Man of Feeling'. The work was published, without this dedication, as *Annals of the Parish; or the Chronicle of Dalmailing;
During the Ministry of the Rev. Micah Balwhidder. Written by
himself. Arranged and Edited by the Author of 'The Ayrshire
Legatees'* at the end of April in Edinburgh and in London by

early May. 'I shall be very much mistaken', wrote Blackwood on
25 April, 'if it is not popular.'

Blackwood was not mistaken. *Annals of the Parish* aroused a
chorus of praise and overnight established Galt's reputation.
Although none of his recent work had carried his name, the secret
— perhaps the parallel to Sir Walter Scott was deliberate — was
no secret. Maga's anonymous review in the May number 'by a
pen second to none in the modern literature of this country' (it
was the Man of Feeling himself, who was well in the secret) after
a long analysis offered 'sincere and candid approbation'. Maga
could hardly expect any other treatment of what it admitted was
work by 'a known contributor'. But equal approbation came from
all quarters. One of the earliest appeared in the *Inverness Courier*
of 10 May, written (according to Blackwood) 'by my friend Mr
Johnstone'. It was a review of penetrating skill. The reviewer saw
the parallel to *The Vicar of Wakefield* and acutely noted that
'Micah Balwhidder is among our modern historians what Wilkie
is among the Scottish painters'. Blackwood was in error on the
authorship of the article. The author was Johnstone's wife,[4] and
she was to reappear years later as the *dea ex machina* at a moment
when Galt really needed appreciation. Other, more widely read,
journals joined the chorus. The solemn *Quarterly Review* in April,
the London popular weekly *John Bull* in May, the *Edinburgh
Monthly Review* in July formed the start of an enthusiastic series
of appreciations that became the general verdict. The work was
still being highly praised in the journals of the following year, in
the *Literary Gazette* of June 1822, in the *Monthly Magazine* in
September, and the series was given its final imprimatur in a
notable article by Jeffrey in the *Edinburgh Review* of October
1823. Galt had written his first masterpiece; and its quality was
immediately recognized.

5

In *Annals of the Parish* Galt dug deep into the memories of his
Ayrshire boyhood. 'Dalmailing' — the parish of the book — he
later identified in his *Literary Life* with the actual village of
Dreghorn, like Dr Pringle's 'Garnock' only a few miles distant
from his birthplace in Irvine ('Irville'). Superimposed on these

earlier memories lay much of his later experiences. While he was
'very young', he recounts in his *Autobiography*, he had hoped
one day 'to write a book that would be for Scotland what the
Vicar of Wakefield is for England'. Some few years later, before
he left Greenock in 1804, a walk in the neighbouring village of
Inverkip drew to his attention the great changes and 'improvements' that the late eighteenth century had brought to rural life.
The first 1813 draft of *The Pastor* established his framework. the
work would be a 'chronicle' of the year-by-year life of a small
Scottish village in the half-century after 1760; the narrator an
elderly man, Micah Balwhidder, recounting his fifty years as
pastor of the parish. It would have the humour and the sharp
realism of Wilkie's paintings, but done in the spoken idiom of the
country.

Galt had already, in *The Ayrshire Legatees*, shown himself to
be a master of character-portrayal of village life. To this he adds
in the final 1821 version of the *Annals* what his business life had
taught him, a knowledge that even an isolated village is not
isolated from the great world, of which it is a part; and a quite
remarkable sense of the impact of social and economic change on
eighteenth-century rural Scotland. Dalmailing is a village of a
few hundred souls, but Galt encapsulates within it the whole
range of human experience. It is a small place and yet — though
newspapers are unknown until half way through its chronicle —
it is at the centre of a whole world. The young men grow up and
become officers in the navy or sail in trading ships to the West
Indies; they join the army when the American colonies rebel;
they are affected by the French Revolution, read 'a daily London
newspaper' in the new bookshop, and are suspected of 'high
treason', but when Boney threatens they form — as Galt did
himself — a loyal corps of sharp-shooters; from the world of
fashion, Lord Eglesham descends from his town house in London,
bringing London wines and a London mistress.

In skilful and unobtrusive touches, Galt pencils in the increasing prosperity of the eighteenth century. Farming methods improve; plantations of timber grow where there had been bare
moorland; the West India trade brings sugar and 'the fashion to
make jam and jelly, which hitherto had been only known in the
kitchens and confectionaries of the gentry'; new imports — and

new ideas — effect changes; the wealthy colonist, Mr Cayenne, arrives and sets up a cotton-mill and finally a new town, full of 'democratical' weavers 'with their liberty and equality principles'; a new turnpike-road is built, which brings 'one of the greatest conveniences' a stage-coach to Glasgow, much to the profit of the second Mrs Balwhidder who increased the market for her butter, 'for the Glasgow merchants are fond of excellent eatables, and the payment was aye ready money'.

As in *The Ayrshire Legatees* and *The Steam-Boat*, the small world and the great world are counterpointed against each other, but in this book Dalmailing is firmly in the centre, and Galt's sly irony of the earlier two books is replaced by a warm-hearted acceptance of the inhabitants of the small world, recorded with humanity and humour. Galt is curiously ambivalent about Dalmailing. He saw the advantages of 'the spirit of improvement, which is so busy everywhere', but the old minister, one if not two generations behind the times, he portrayed with affection and admiration, one side of Galt sympathizing with his lament 'in the midst of all this commercing and manufacturing, I began to discover signs of decay in the wonted simplicity of our country ways'.

Annals of the Parish has no plot. Its coherence lies in the unity of theme, the continuity of the central characters, and Galt's undeviating ability to write through the eyes — and in the language — of his chosen persona, the elderly Micah Balwhidder. This, with the chronicle framework — and Blackwood's 'gentle pruning' — disciplined Galt's tendency to fragmentary and 'clishmaclaver' construction, and the whole is a considerable piece of writing. Galt in the 'Reflections on my own works' in his *Autobiography*, written when the *Annals* had already attained the status of a classic, denied that it (or any of his books of this time) conforms to the popular conception of a novel: a novel needs 'a consistent fable' — 'in the Annals of the Parish there is nothing that properly deserves to be regarded as a story'. What he claimed to be writing — and in this he saw himself as a pioneer — were 'theoretical histories of society, limited . . . necessarily to the events of a circumscribed locality'. But the *Annals* — and the best of Galt's work of this period — were more than that; they had at their core that exploration and exposition of

inter-relationship between person and person which is the real
heart of the novel. What Galt had done in fact was not merely
to create a masterpiece; he has expanded the whole scope of the
Novel.

The quiet art of the *Annals* has a quite deceptive simplicity.
Galt writes with affection of a Scotland that was vanishing. But
there is no romantic nostalgia for the past, no glamour, no senti-
mentality. Dalmailing has its fornicators as well as its romantic
lovers; the sound Christian doctrine and humanity of Mr
Balwhidder cannot prevent either a murder or a suicide; his
presbyterian piety can co-exist quite happily with his second
wife's ability to make 'siller like sclate stanes', turning the Manse
into 'a factory of butter and cheese'. Blackwood reported that the
Professor said it was 'not a book but a fact' and followed this up
(25 June) with an account of his 'worthy old Mother' who
thought 'Micah an honest and upright minister of the gospel'
but being told by one of her grandchildren that the book was a
novel, was very angry at having been deceived. In the present
century, the historian G. M. Trevelyan, seeking to illustrate the
period in his *English Social History*, by-passes the genuine documents of the time and cites instead *Annals of the Parish*, 'which
still remains the most intimate and human picture of Scotland
during her period of change in the reign of George III'.[5] Like
Defoe's *Journal of the Plague Year*, *Annals of the Parish* is more
real than the real thing. Both are nevertheless works of fiction,
transcending mere social documentation, and the products of
great art.

Perhaps the most remarkable aspect of Galt's immediate success was his simultaneous acceptance both north and south of the
border. *Annals of the Parish* was written uncompromisingly in
West of Scotland dialect. It is true that by 1821 Sir Walter Scott
had made Scottish novels acceptable, but Scott provided plenty
of romantic adventure and unceasing narrative interest. Galt
offered neither. Yet Blackwood on 20 May, a few days after the
London publication, heard from Cadell 'that the *Annals* were
very popular, and were selling well'. The London weekly *John
Bull* (no great enthusiast for dialect writing) announced on 13 May
that the *Annals* 'bears strong marks of genius and talent, and we
strongly recommend it to our readers'. Blackwood by the end of

the year felt impelled to send Galt twenty guineas, supplementary
to the original sixty. Even in February of the following year, just
before the second edition appeared, Cadell (as Blackwood reported on 5 March 1822) sold over four hundred copies in a few
days at one of his London sales. If Galt had laid down his pen in
May 1821, his reputation was secured.

4. The years with Blackwood
II: The crest of the wave

1

GALT HAD no intention of laying down his pen. In the early months of 1821, in addition to seeing the *Annals* through the press, he was driving ahead with three further books for Blackwood. The first of these was no great burden, being the revision from the pages of the magazine of *The Ayrshire Legatees* for issue in one volume. The last monthly instalment had barely appeared when Galt wrote Blackwood on 28 February reminding him of his earlier proposal to have the whole 'printed separately'. Galt had already come to see that the *Legatees*, the *Annals*, and the still unwritten *Steam-Boat*, with their characters and incidents interlocking from book to book and a unified Garnock-Dalmailing-Irvine-Glasgow setting, were no more than sequent volumes in a single coherent 'theoretical history'. He proposed, therefore, that Blackwood in republishing *The Ayrshire Legatees* should bring it out as the first part of a 'general work' for which he proposed the title *Tales of the West* — 'the Parish Annals would belong to the series and also Mr Duffle's travels' — and also, (he could have added) four more titles of which Blackwood had as yet no warning. Galt was, in fact, creating the first *roman fleuve*.

Blackwood 'thought a good deal about this' and diplomatically delayed his reply. *Tales of a Landlord* was an obvious parallel — but Blackwood had no reason to like *that* series. When he did reply on 20 May he had read the first enthusiastic reviews of *Annals of the Parish* and these convinced him that a 'general title was rather a disadvantage' . . . after a few more books, perhaps, 'but in the mean time you may rest assured, it is much better that each single volume should seem to be complete in itself and not be inseparable from the others'. Blackwood published

41

this single volume on 13 June, *The Ayrshire Legatees or The Pringle Family By the Author of 'Annals of the Parish'*. Galt in his revision made some slight verbal alterations, eliminated an intermediary narrator (Mr McGruel, the Kilwinning doctor), wrote some new linking passages, and generally tightened up the book. He wanted to 'rescue' the Responsive Notices, but Blackwood preferred the revised text without them. The recent success and publicity of the *Annals* brought an immediate new audience for the republished version of the *Legatees*, so that *John Bull* in London could announce on 1 July as a complete recommendation simply 'We intended noticing "The Ayrshire Legatees" but this we find to be unnecessary, as its merits are already appreciated'.

Galt's second project for the year was put to Blackwood on 30 January — 'were I to get sufficient encouragement I think I could write a novel, on the progress of a Scotchman in London'. Blackwood made no encouraging counter-move, and Galt on 14 February told him 'as my public business is now coming on, I shall have but little time for literature'. There is, in the Colonial Office papers in the Public Record Office,[1] evidence that Galt had indeed already begun with some vigour his campaign of interviewing officials and writing considerable memoranda on behalf of his Canadian clients. By May he was, in addition, engaged to pilot two private bills through the House on behalf of churches in Scotland[2] and this meant interviewing members. But already by 27 February, having 'got hold of a proper hero' he had begun his 'Scotchman's progress' as a 'work of leisure'. By 18 April 'any leisure I have at present is chiefly devoted to the Scottish hero in London, for the subject has taken possession of my imagination'.

Blackwood knew that another Tale of the West was on the way and decided to intervene. Galt was one of his best-sellers. Here was the chance to challenge Sir Walter Scott and get from Galt something different — a really long novel with a good plot. 'A great matter,' he wrote on 25 April, 'is to construct a good and striking story with which to interweave your graphic sketches of actual life and manners.' To this advice Galt offered no comment. The big novel with the good and striking story was something he had so far not written with any success. He simply laid aside his Scotchman's progress for the moment and put up a new plan,

The Provost, to Blackwood, who replied enthusiastically on 20 May 'Provost Hookie . . . is a glorious subject'; and Galt a week later was able to reassure him that 'The Provost is in a thriving way'. Thereafter for the summer months of 1821 (Parliament being in recess) Galt was writing, in addition to some of the best episodes of *The Steam-Boat*, portions of *The Provost* and the Scotchman's progress, which had now acquired the title *Sir Andrew Wylie*. He even found time to do a review 'On the Saxon Chronicle' in the June number of his old stand-by, the *Monthly Magazine*. By 30 July he was able to send off his triumphant episode of Mr Duffle at the Coronation, and announce that *Sir Andrew Wylie* was 'now two thirds written'. *The Provost* he would suspend meanwhile and devote his whole time to *Sir Andrew Wylie* — for which John Murray had offered five hundred guineas. 'If you like I will send you the first volume to look at.'

Blackwood lost no further time. He had not seen a page of the novel, but the August number of the magazine announced 'We have much pleasure in informing our readers, that the author of "The Ayrshire Legatees", and "Annals of the Parish", is preparing a Scottish novel for the press, which he intends to call "Sir Andrew Wylie of that Ilk"'. Galt decided his best plan was to leave his family in London and move to Edinburgh to finish the writing. There he stayed with Blackwood's brother.[3] Blackwood, now that he had Galt safely at hand, did not — in spite of his London rival's five hundred guineas — hasten to conclude the deal. On 8 September Galt, now in Edinburgh, was given an eighteen-month bill 'to account', for *Sir Andrew Wylie*, *The Provost*, and magazine articles, the terms and conditions 'to be afterwards adjusted'. The final adjustment did not come till Galt had been writing in Edinburgh for four months, when on 29 December he accepted £200 for *Sir Andrew Wylie*, plus a further £200 to be paid when Blackwood had sold 1500 copies. For *The Provost* he received at the same time 100 guineas. In all, Blackwood paid him £480 between August and the end of the year. It is true that, of this total, £305 was for *The Provost*, not yet written, and for *Sir Andrew Wylie*, not completed till the end of January. The remainder was for contributions already printed in the magazine. But the copy of the accounts[4] which is attached

to Galt's letter of acceptance reveals that only £25 of this grand
total was paid in cash. The remaining £455 was in three bills not
due for at least a twelvemonth. There were not one but two
canny Scots in the venture, and the paymaster could call the tune.

2

Call the tune was precisely what Blackwood did, now that he had
Galt at hand and a family guest. During his months in Edinburgh,
Galt worked full-time for Blackwood. He produced five lengthy
contributions for Maga, which appeared in the September,
October, November and December issues; he wrote a com-
mendatory preface (dated 12 December) for a Blackwood book,
Memoirs of a Life chiefly passed in Pennsylvania; and he was set
down to do a complete revision and expansion of *Sir Andrew
Wylie*. Blackwood had already provided the right title for *Annals
of the Parish* and had submitted its original text to 'a gentle
pruning'. As the publisher of a successful magazine he had some
idea of what the public wanted. The manuscript of *Sir Andrew
Wylie* that Galt brought to Edinburgh was not the novel Blackwood had in mind, and he set his virtually captive author to
expand and rewrite it, delaying the final settlement of the contract
until he had got what he wanted.

Galt some years later in his *Literary Life* was to record 'I repine
at the change I was induced to make in my original'. From the
evidence of the two autobiographical books and the letters, it is
clear that *Sir Andrew Wylie* was originally planned as a third
study in the Garnock-Dalmailing series. For his new novel, Galt
created a third village, Stoneyholm, on the outskirts of Irvine, the
birthplace of an orphan boy brought up by a grandmother. The
boyhood mirrored Galt's own. The hero goes to London as a
young man, and he was depicted as a blunt-speaking Scot who
contrived to get on in the world, rising ever higher in the profession of law, moving ever higher in the social scale as he becomes
the intimate of politicians and aristocrats. 'No particular story is
engrafted on my original idea' — the original *Sir Andrew Wylie*
was, like the *Annals* and *The Ayrshire Legatees*, planned as a
series of episodes in Ayrshire and London illustrating 'the rise and
progress of a humble Scotchman'. When Galt wrote to Black-

wood on 30 July 1821 before he arrived in Edinburgh, all that remained to be completed of his planned novel was 'the hero's return to his native land and final settling in his estate'.

What emerged after Blackwood's insistence on 'a good and striking story' was something different, a three-volume novel, crammed with incidents described afterwards by Galt as 'too romantic and uncommon for my taste'. It contained not one story but three intertwined narratives — Galt was giving full value for money. Blackwood got what he wanted, a novel that the public would buy with something in it for everybody. The first edition was published at the end of January 1822, *Sir Andrew Wylie of that Ilk by the Author of 'Annals of the Parish'*, etc., priced at a guinea, a considerable increase on the eight-shilling *Annals* and the seven-shilling *Legatees*. The 1500 copies sold rapidly, and a second edition was required by July of the same year. It was not yet Sir Walter Scott's level of sales; but for Blackwood it was the right direction.

Galt, however, having completed his task, left Edinburgh in late January 1822 with suppressed resentment. The 'interference' (as he was afterwards to call it) with his planned novel rankled; and the deferment of his payment was a hardship. He had returned to his family and his political activity and he required ready money for both. He appealed to his father-in-law for an advance of £200 and, taking a chance that his credit with his publisher was good, provided Dr Tilloch with a draft on Blackwood at 14 months, judging (rightly as it turned out) that well before that time the 1500 copies would be sold and the second £200 for *Sir Andrew Wylie* would be available to meet the draft. Blackwood in a cool letter on 2 March was 'not a little surprised' and refused to accept the draft. However a few days later he had second thoughts, and on 8 March wrote Dr Tilloch, saying that since the sale of the novel 'is continuing to go on' he would very soon 'return the bill accepted'. The incident was seemingly closed, but it was remembered on both sides. Galt thought that Blackwood's treatment had been shabby; Blackwood thought that his author had tried to force his hand.

Sir Andrew Wylie is, as a result, a long patchwork novel that can shift from mere competence to excellence as the reader crosses the lines of cleavage between one layer of writing and another.

There are arbitrary changes in direction and tone that result in
the parts being better than the whole. Four separate strands can
be readily detected. The first is the original story, admirably
handled in the language and manner of his recent successes, the
Annals and *The Ayrshire Legatees*. The early chapters on the
poor orphan Wylie's (and Galt's) Ayrshire boyhood and his
arrival as a young man in London are excellent. After a successful career in London and many adventures (only a few of them
likely to have been part of the original story) Wylie returns a
wealthy man to his birthplace, and in the long concluding section
(which made up most of the third volume, now chapters lxxx–cv
of the one-volume edition) his newly-acquired baronetcy and
Ayrshire landed estate wins him a grudging acceptance by the old
Tory Laird of Craiglands as a fit husband for his daughter. In all
this, the third part of his 'theoretical history' of the rural west of
Scotland, Galt scores a notable success and further extends the
Garnock-Dalmailing gallery in the person of the self-possessed
Wylie himself, the die-hard Laird of Craiglands, his spinster
sister Miss Mizy, and a whole new group of minor but memorable
characters. By the end of the novel, Galt came to see that in the
old Laird he had created a central character for a further novel,
and concluded with a promise to his public of the Laird's own
account 'anent the decay of the ancient families of the west
country'. It was to be written some years later as *The Last of the
Lairds*, Galt's final novel of his years with Blackwood.

The second section was originally meant to be a plotless series
of encounters between Wylie and each of his new English friends
and acquaintances, all illustrating his broad — and blunt —
Scots tongue and his upward progress. Wylie's earliest encounter
was with Lord Sandyford — an aristocrat modelled on Galt's
friend Lord Blessington — who becomes Wylie's patron. However, the demand for a 'good and striking story' caused this part
to be extended greatly, and Galt (with memories of his earlier
aristocratic friend Lord Byron) evolved a complex and romantic
plot involving the separation of Lord and Lady Sandyford, she
wrongfully accused of infidelity, her retreat to a Radcliffean
castle, and their ultimate reunion through Wylie's busy agency.

The third section is pure patchwork. Had Galt not been under
Blackwood's pressure 'there would certainly', he notes in his

Autobiography, 'have been no such episode as the gypsies introduced'. It is essentially a separate story (chapters xlv–lvi) which can be excised without affecting the continuity of the novel. Wylie, on a visit to his patron, meets a group of gypsies, two of whom are later accused of a murder. Wylie (suspecting the real murderer) engages a lawyer to defend them and (with Lord Sandyford on the bench) the section concludes with a dramatic court-room scene. The whole section, detachable though it may be from the body of the novel, is tightly and dramatically written. It is one of the earliest examples in English of the murder-and-detection genre, and it is no wonder that many contemporary readers found it 'the best contrived part of the narrative'.

In the fourth section, Galt again breaks new ground, both for himself and for the English novel. Wylie's success with the Sandyfords brings him to the attention of a Duke-of-Omnium-like figure, the Marquis of Avonside, who offers him a pocket borough. Wylie accepts, on his own terms, wins the election (with some assistance from the gypsies from section three) and proves himself a shrewd committee man in the House. His political services bring him the baronetcy that ensured his return to Ayrshire would (like Dr Pringle's) be a triumphant progress. Galt was himself an outsider in the world of politics; but he was at the time walking the corridors of power, and the succession of political discussions, jobbery, grand dinners, royal levees, and string-pulling behind the scenes is expertly done and new to English fiction. Galt in this section is a pioneer. While Disraeli and Trollope were still schoolboys, he was quietly initiating the political novel.

The final judgment on *Sir Andrew Wylie* cannot fail to be a mixed one. When Galt is creating on a basis of what he knows, he writes with vigour and insight. The Scottish and political scenes are brilliant. Blackwood's interference prevented the novel from having the artistic unity of the two earlier books. On the other hand, his shrewd appraisal of what the public wanted ensured that Galt wrote a book readily accepted in his own time. It was widely reviewed and sold well and elevated Galt's status in London circles. The second edition was dedicated to Lord Blessington; Galt made overtures to present a copy of the first edition to the King, and on 18 May was able to tell Blackwood that the librarian at Carlton House had been 'directed to express

. . . his Majesty's gratification'; in June his political business made such progress that he was presented in Court and on 15 June he wrote that his reception had been 'considered a particularly gracious one, in consequence of the King speaking to me . . . so much perhaps for Sir Andrew'. It may not have been the book he intended to write, but he could not deny Blackwood's shrewdness.

3

Back in London, Galt busily resumed his 'parliamentary visitations'. He still had on his hands the Church bills from the previous session and the agency for his Canadian clients; a Corn Bill that affected their interests had to be watched. This occupied many of his daylight hours till June, when his Canadian business appeared to have reached a satisfactory settlement. But he was in London only a few days when a letter from Blackwood of 6 February arrived, to remind him of no fewer than three works promised: the revision of *The Steam-Boat* for volume publication; the completion of *The Provost*, which Blackwood with utter confidence had advertised in January at the end of the third volume of *Sir Andrew Wylie* as 'preparing for publication'; and a series of 'Letters from Westminster' for the magazine.

Galt had enough memoranda of an official nature to write for Westminster (and probably some discreet second thoughts on this last promise) and the first five numbers of Maga in 1822 contained no Galt article on this or any other topic. 'The poor lady', wrote Blackwood on 23 March, 'might have been dead and buried for anything you seem to have cared these some months past.' Even in the form of a ponderous joke, this complaint was pretty unreasonable. Galt, in his 'leisure' from public duties, was pressing ahead at speed with work for Blackwood. In February, he was involved in the second edition of the *Annals*, which appeared in March. Between February and April he completed *The Provost*, sending it off to Edinburgh in 'portions'. It was published in May. He did at intervals a thorough revision, amounting to a complete re-writing, of *The Steam-Boat*, and had the last part off his hands by June. It was published in July. The 1500 copies of *Sir Andrew Wylie* being nearly exhausted, Blackwood, deserting his usual Edinburgh printers, had the second edition printed by

A. and R. Spottiswoode in London. This meant that Galt took over the entire responsibility for supervising proofs in May and in June for its publication in early July. In May he completed a review of a book by Lord Aberdeen which appeared as an article, 'Greek Architecture — Lord Aberdeen' signed by his old *nom-de-plume* 'Viator', in the June number of Maga. In May and June he sent Blackwood two long stories for a new series tentatively entitled *The Quarantine*. He might be easing off on contributions written specifically for the magazine; he was not neglecting Blackwood.

During these months, Galt produced excellent work, including his biggest immediate success. This did not prevent a feeling getting abroad that he was writing too much. His recent record of books published had certainly been astonishing: in January the three-volume *Sir Andrew Wylie*; in March the second edition of the *Annals*; in May *The Provost*; in June its second edition; in July *The Steam-Boat*; in the same month the second edition of *Sir Andrew Wylie*. Not all of this was new. The majority of the volumes were reprints or revision of older work. But the total was nevertheless ten volumes in seven months and a certain querulous tone began to creep into the reviews. The *Quarterly Review*, which the previous year had been 'pleased and affected by the Chronicle of Dalmailing', went out of its way in the issue of January 1822 to call Galt 'a person, to say the best of it, of a very uncertain taste'. Galt laughed this off to Blackwood (14 March) as 'the critique of Old Maggy'. But the friendly *Monthly Review* in May, commending highly *Sir Andrew Wylie* and noting that *The Provost* had just appeared, applauded Galt's 'powers of fertility', yet felt it should utter a word of warning — 'It may, perhaps, be well soon to commit his pen to prison'. Success, in the competitive literary world, had its attendant dangers; and even Blackwood, ever sensitive to public reaction, was soon to wonder if he was not pressing his author too much.

There was, however, no question about the instant success of *The Provost by the Author of Annals of the Parish; Ayrshire Legatees; and Sir Andrew Wylie*, published in May in an edition of 2000. Maga reported the following month that the whole edition sold in a fortnight and a second edition of the same size was melting away 'like snaw aff a dyke'. Some reviews ran counter to the public approval and echoed the recent disquiet concerning Galt's over-productivity — 'this indefatigable writer' was the comment of the *Monthly Review*, in its September notice. But the reception of *The Provost*, even when a reviewer was not entirely in sympathy with the enthusiastic purchasers of this particular volume, established Galt finally as an author who merited not just a notice of each single book but a serious critical consideration on the basis of an established body of writing. The London *Literary Gazette* of 22 June 1822 significantly headed its six-column review of *The Provost* 'Mr Galt's Novels' and made it the opportunity for a full-scale appreciation of an author 'deservedly held in very high estimation' who is 'like one of the Flemish masters'. Another man who was like one of the Flemish masters took the hint. The arrest in chapter xxxvi of the strolling player, a 'termagant woman', by the town officers is the basis of Wilkie's 'The Parish Beadle', painted shortly afterwards.

The Provost is a brilliant fusion of the two elements which, separately, had given strength to *Sir Andrew Wylie*, the small-town Scottish scene and the world of political action. Galt, ever since his early reading of Machiavelli, had been fascinated by the shrewd exercise of political power. During his London years he had seen it at work. His birthplace, the self-governing royal borough of Irvine, the 'Gudetown' of the novel, was large enough for political action, small enough to be displayed as a microcosm of the greater world beyond. The central character and narrator, James Pawkie, recounts his career in town politics over the same period of years as Dr Balwhidder's incumbency of Dalmailing. Once again, Galt chronicles the progress of a Scottish town in the later eighteenth century, this time from the point of view of a sly ('pawkie') tradesman who himself progresses from his apprentice-ship to his own shop and then ownership of a row of houses, from a seat on the town council, where he soon learned 'to rule without being felt, which is the great mystery of policy', to the lucrative office of Dean of Guild, and finally to the supreme office of Provost, to which he contrived to be three times elected at strate-gic intervals, ensuring that both in office and in the intervening periods 'I was enabled to wind the council round my finger'.

Of all Galt's theoretical histories, *The Provost* is the most tightly constructed. There are no loose ends, no digressions, no alien interpolated passages. The self-told, self-revealing narrative moves steadily from young Pawkie's prudent choice of a profitable trade right to his masterly organizing as an old man of the vote of thanks and the 'very handsome silver cup, bearing an inscription in the Latin tongue' with which the council rewarded his service to Gudetown. He manipulates everybody and everything, the council, the corps of volunteers, the gentry, the local Member of Parliament, the newspaper, the traffic and the progress of the town. He can be kind; he is never ruthless. With grave decorum he feathers his own nest: public contracts contrive to effect improvements on or near his own properties; it is his shop that provides the uniforms for the volunteers — 'I must confess', he writes, 'with a sort of sinister respect for my own interest'. But as he grows older (and wealthier) he 'had less incitement to be so grippy', and with a clear conscience he can become a reformer and can move (and insist on others moving) 'to partake of the purer spirit which the great mutations of the age had conjured into public affairs'.

The initial immediate success of *The Provost* was unquestionably due to its being accepted as a work of rich comedy. Its permanent value lies not so much in the succession of comic scenes as in Galt's subtle and ironic study in self-revelation. It is comedy with serious overtones not recognized by many of his early readers, who mainly saw in it a further instalment of Scots dialect humour. There was one subtle critic of the time who did recognize what Galt had achieved. Coleridge, in Highgate, bought the first edition of *The Provost* when it appeared, and this induced him to buy more of Galt. His judgment remained unrecorded until his copy of *The Provost* turned up some years ago, with a typical magistral note in his hand-writing:

'This work is not for the Many; but in the unconscious, perfectly natural, Irony of Self-delusion, in all parts intelligible to the intelligent Reader, without the slightest suspicion on the part of the Autobiographer, I know of no equal in our Literature. The governing Trait in the Provost's character is no where caricatured. In the character of Betty, John's wife, or the Beggar Girl intense Selfishness without malignity, as a *Nature*, and with all the innocence of a Nature, is admirably pourtrayed. In the Provost a similar *Selfness* is united with a *Slyness* and a

plausibility eminently successful in cheating the man himself
into a happy state of constant Self-applause. This and "The
Entail" would alone suffice to place Galt in the first rank of
contemporary Novellists — and second only to Sir W. Scott in
technique.'[5]

To sell 4000 copies of *The Provost* in a few months was a
popular success that Galt (and Blackwood) appreciated to the
full. Every author hopes that his books will sell. Yet in the end
what he needs is a different kind of approbation. When an older
Galt came to assess his work critically in his *Literary Life*, the two
books that he singled out were *The Provost* and *The Entail*. 'I,
very simply perhaps, acknowledge that to myself it [*The Provost*]
has always appeared superior to the Annals of the Parish' . . .
'The Entail is considered among my best.' Galt was never to have
the reassurance that would have come from knowing that his own
assessment had already been confirmed by the greatest critic of
the age. Coleridge, and perhaps only Coleridge in his own day,
had penetrated to the very heart of his achievement.

In the middle of 1822, however, Galt still saw his future in the
world of affairs. He was less concerned with absolute judgments
on his books than with their immediate sales and the consequent
effect on his public standing. His confidence in himself as a public
figure mounted with each successive book, and the nature of his
ambitions at this time may be charted with some accuracy from
his dedications. *The Ayrshire Legatees* he had inscribed to his old
business principal, Kirkman Finlay of Glasgow. His literary
principal he acknowledged by dedicating the second edition of
the *Annals* to Christopher North. These debts paid, he turned to
the world of his wider aspirations. *The Provost* was inscribed to a
friendly member of the government, the Hon. Robert Downie,
M.P., of Appin, and then raising his sights he followed this with
dedications to noblemen of his acquaintance, *Sir Andrew Wylie*
to Lord Blessington and *The Steam-Boat* to Lord Gwydyr. When
his writing and proof-reading for June was completed, he turned
with barely a week's delay to his next novel *The Entail*. It was to
be his major work; and it was to be dedicated, by royal permission, to George IV. A royal acceptance of a dedication was no
literary accolade. But it conferred what Galt really wanted,
recognition of his standing.

5. The years with Blackwood
III: Triumph and retreat

1

GALT IN June 1822 was on the crest of a wave. Everything was going well. His books were selling. His Canadian negotiations were proceeding. The King had been gracious. As if to seal his triumph, Christopher North decided the time had come to 'reveal' the secret of his authorship. The occasion offered was a long letter by E. E. Crowe, an 'occasional contributor', in the June number of Maga in which as 'Francis Freeman', discussing a group of recent Blackwood publications, he openly praised Galt and defended him against the criticism of the *Quarterly Review*. 'C.N.' used the opportunity to append a biographical and critical article on Galt, whom he described as 'a modest man of indisputable and rare genius', and firmly identified him as 'the sole author' of the recent series.

The immediate response was a letter signed 'Philomag', defending the *Quarterly* and objecting to the 'outrageous eulogy on one Mr Galt — a small author, with a small talent in one small way, but out of that small line, the longest, lankest, blindest, dullest haberdasher of prose, which even our prosing day can produce'. This letter was printed in the July number and was manfully answered and rebutted by Christopher North, blow answering blow in parallel columns in the free hard-hitting manner of the period. The exchange reads more like a battle of abuse between supporters of rival journals and publishers than considered criticism on either side. Christopher North assumed that 'Philomag' was J. W. Croker, one of the stalwarts of the *Quarterly*. This is possible. The evidence is simply lacking. The 'Philomag' letter is couched in such intemperate language and its every point is so neatly and knowledgeably rebutted by Christopher North that one suspects the whole thing may well be an inside job: the Blackwood team campaigning for a Blackwood author. It would not have been their first fabrication.

The immediate result was certainly increased sales for Galt, and he settled down to plan his next novel, *The Entail*, in a mood of confidence, his letters to Blackwood in June and July recording its rapid early progress. 'During the summer', he wrote on 8 June, 'I intend to devote myself exclusively to "The Entail" which I foresee will extend to three volumes, the scene will be altogether in Scotland — Edinburgh will come in, but the chief business lies in Glasgow.' By 15 June he told the astonished Blackwood to announce it — 'I am sure that these early announcements do good, the very fecundity becomes an advertising topic'. Finding the libraries on the south coast well stocked with his novels, on 23 June Galt wrote that this had given him 'renewed heart and confidence, in so much that I have constructed the whole fable of my Entail, determined the characters and most of the incidents — I may be mistaken in my anticipation, but I think it will be out of all comparison the most vigorous and lively work I have yet attempted. . . . The story will grasp nearly a century, as it comprehends three generations and in so far will embrace a great deal of matter similar in compass to the annals and the provost besides being complete as a dramatic plot within itself.'

Blackwood could hardly overlook the recent grumbles about Galt's productivity — 'folks are apt to say you are in too great hurry', he replied on 22 June. But he could also hardly forget that he had five Galt novels on his list, all currently selling; and in the June number of Maga — in spite of his 'doughts as to the propriety of announcing *The Entail* so soon after *The Provost*' — he ran a full-page advertisement for all five, and announced in large bold type *The Entail* as 'preparing for publication'. If fecundity was an advertising topic, he would play it up for all it was worth.

Galt had two immediate problems on his hands. The first was — as usual — money. On 8 June he made overtures to Blackwood for support and received an encouraging reply by return. Galt then on 23 June announced a new scheme — 'I am anxious to make arrangements for spending three months in Scotland, where I may be enabled to add to my vernacular vocabulary'.

Plate III: D. M. Moir

PLATE IV: Guelph, "one of the towns founded by Mr Galt for the Canada Company in Upper Canada"

Blackwood responded on 28 June with a bill at fifteen months for
£300. On 31 August (Galt having arrived in Edinburgh) he paid
him two further bills, bringing the total to £525, the greatest
sum Galt had received for a book from Blackwod. The publisher
could not have been more prompt, and Galt was able to leave for
Scotland in mid-July. He travelled via Liverpool, where (as he
wrote to Lady Blessington on 27 July) he was negotiating for an
agency, 'a most desirable appendage to my other concerns,' and
found that *Sir Andrew Wylie* had ensured him a 'flattering'
reception.[1] The buoyant mood continued. His writing was producing both cash and public reputation.

Galt's second problem was to prove less tractable. Blackwood
had readily provided the means. Once again he began to call the
tune. His letters to Galt of June and July are full of advice on his
writing. He took violent objection to one of Galt's recently submitted short stories — 'there is something which shocks my feelings', he wrote of one episode. Galt made no comment, and the
story was returned unused. On the proposed (and still unseen)
The Entail Blackwood was even more specific. 'I hope,' he wrote
on 11 June, 'you will be able to manage it so as that the hero tells
the story himself for you may depend upon it, that it is always
the most effective way, and it is particularly your forte. You more
than any one almost I know, identify the individual, and the
Author never himself appears, it is the very being telling his story
himself. This is greatly lost when given in the third person.' When
Galt wrote back, but preserved silence on this point, Blackwood
said it all over again in his letter of 22 June. Galt again made no
comment. He could still remember the effect on *Sir Andrew
Wylie* of Blackwood's demand for 'a good and striking story'. He
took the coach for Scotland, well forewarned that more 'interference' was to be expected.

Galt spent August in Edinburgh. He continued working on
The Entail and by the end of the month had given the printer
most of the manuscript for the first volume. Blackwood, having
Galt on hand, could not refrain from pressing him for an article
for Maga. 'Here', wrote Galt to Lady Blessington on 13 August,
'all are on tip-toe for the King'.[2] To Blackwood, with the success
of Mr Duffle's account of the Coronation in mind, this was a
chance not to be missed and Galt was set to describe the royal

visit of George IV to the northern capital. The result was 'The
Gathering of the West', which filled nearly thirty pages of the
September number. Galt in this long sketch assembles a group of
west of Scotland characters and describes with ironical amuse-
ment their adventures in Edinburgh during the royal visit. Old
friends appear — the Pringles, Sir Andrew Wylie, Mr Duffle,
Mrs Ogle of Balbogle and a host of other characters from his
recent books, and the whole thing is a witty and high-spirited
extension of his *roman-fleuve*. Blackwood had every reason to be
satisfied with Galt's *jeu d'esprit*. Largely because of it, the
September 'royal' number of Maga sold out and a second edition
had to be run off, and early in the following year 'The Gathering
of the West' was twice reprinted in book form.

Galt left Edinburgh immediately after the royal visit. He had
come to Scotland for 'vernacular vocabulary'. The dialect he
wanted to soak himself in was spoken not in Edinburgh but in his
own west country. He had a better chance, too, of completing
The Entail in his own way if he were not too close to Blackwood.
He went to Greenock, joining his mother and sister in the family
house, and settled down to three months of sustained writing. In
intervals of more creative work, he satisfied Blackwood's immediate needs by writing three articles, one on foreign affairs, 'The
Greeks and the Greek Cause', for the October number of Maga,
and two pieces on agricultural economics, 'Hints to the Country
Gentlemen', which appeared in October and November. For
these, signing himself 'Bandana', he adopted the persona of a
Glasgow merchant. Considering his current pre-occupation in
The Entail, he could hardly have adopted any other.

As early as 23 June, Galt, in London, had promised Blackwood
to have *The Entail* 'ready before Christmas for the public'.
Settled in Greenock, he made steady and uninterrupted progress
and on 3 September wrote for proofs of his first volume. On
8 October he asked Blackwood for 'the Entail made up as far as
the matter goes — for I wish the second volume to begin with the
commencement of a new act in the story — and may have occasion to write a chapter or two to extend the first.' He was planning, with the sophisticated calculation of a Jane Austen, the
dramatic structure of his novel in terms of the volume division.
By 11 October he was able to report that he had 'a considerable

portion of Vol. II ready'. The end was in sight of a long novel which he had determinedly written in his own way.

Galt was not to succeed in this intention. The third volume shows an abrupt change of tone and contains considerable material alien to the run of the earlier narrative. No letters survive from the weeks of its composition. Probably none were written, since Galt visited Edinburgh in the middle of October, bringing with him what he had completed, and author and publisher could discuss the concluding section of the novel face to face. There does exist an angry letter, written some years later (23 August 1826), in which Galt set out a list of Blackwood's interventions in his novels, culminating in the blunt statement 'the main fault of the Entail was owing to my being over-persuaded . . . I cannot proceed if I am interfered with'.

It is clear that Blackwood returned to his old insistence, pressing his author to fill out the third volume with the kind of incident he called 'striking'. Galt completed the book under some duress. The final chapters he did manage to write in the tone and manner he intended, but his planned structure had been disrupted. When, in the middle of all this, Galt ventured to raise the question of his *next* book — and some payment for it — Blackwood took alarm and told him he had been publishing too rapidly; he did not 'wish him to bring out any other Book for nearly 12 months'. Galt hastily put *The Entail* through the press, added the royal dedication (printed last with the other preliminaries) on 3 December, and returned to London and political business. He brought with him in his baggage a speedily prepared copy, specially bound in the 'royal' manner, and it was conveyed to George IV. The acknowledgement was 'most pleasing'. On 11 December he saw the first batch of copies of *The Entail or The Lairds of Grippy by the Author of Annals of the Parish, Sir Andrew Wylie etc.* arrive for sale in the bookseller Richardson's shop. Galt had kept his promised timetable, his major novel, in three volumes dedicated to the King, completed 'before Christmas for the public'. But he was utterly put out by what had taken place in Edinburgh and was quietly smouldering with resentment.

2

In *The Entail or The Lairds of Grippy* Galt expanded his scene
from the small Ayrshire town to commercial Glasgow of the
eighteenth century. The orphan, Claud Walkinshaw, grows up in
the city in poverty, and after twenty years as a pedlar returns a
successful cloth-merchant. At the age of forty-seven, now wealthy,
he marries the daughter of the laird of the Ayrshire estate of
Plealands. Three sons and a daughter are born. Claud's obsession
with repossessing the lands lost by his grandfather leads him to
acquire the farm of the Grippy, which he entails on his eldest son
Charles. Plealands in due course is inherited by the second son,
Watty, a half-wit. Claud greedily seizes the opportunity to combine the two estates into one sizeable family property. Since he
cannot disinherit Watty from Plealands, he ruthlessly joins it to
the Grippy, entailed on Watty and his male heirs, and disinherits
his elder son.

Galt sets his stage in the opening ten chapters. The remainder
of the three volumes relentlessly pursues Claud's obsession with
'heirs-male and gear' — family name and property. He assembles
the old Walkinshaw estate, reassured in his decision when Charles
makes a romantic and imprudent match. Watty is cajoled into
marriage; the wife dies in childbirth, leaving a daughter, and
Claud's hope of male succession to the entail is ended. Blow
follows blow: Charles dies; Watty relapses to idiocy. Claud,
broken, — 'I sowed tares, and maunna expek wheat' — prepares
a settlement for Charles' widow and children but his corrosive
meanness has affected his wife and she frustrates the dying man's
only good deed, in a scene (vol. ii, chap. xi) which for irony and
horror has few equals in literature. Galt — in Greenock — was
writing at the height of his powers.

This scene is the turning-point of the novel. Greed and meanness slowly give way to light. Claud's widow 'the Leddy', hitherto
only a chattel, emerges as a powerful, loquacious, and warmly
human matriarch. The third son, a ruthless merchant like his
father, has Watty declared insane, becomes the next laird of
Grippy, and pensions off his mother meanly in a flat 'up the dirty
turnpike stairs o' Glasgow'. When he perishes — his death by

shipwreck is one of the intrusive 'striking' incidents of the third volume — the estate passes illegally to the daughter. But the resourceful Leddy finally triumphs — 'ye maun understand that I hae some knowledge o' what pertains to law' — and restores the estate to the rightful heir, the son of Charles.

Within this powerful and dramatic framework, Galt creates his most remarkable novel. *The Entail* is a further instalment of his 'theoretical history' of the west of Scotland, developing over a century of trade from rural simplicity to economic power. This, as Galt the economist and businessman knew, was progress. But it can corrupt the human heart. Galt never forgets that what he is writing is not a treatise but a novel. The protagonists are self-revealed, in Galt's assured manner. The control of narrative and dialogue is masterly. Scenes like the death of Claud, poor Watty's comic yet tender wooing, his court-appearance when he is legally declared an idiot, the Leddy's bursts of unflagging rhetoric, remain in the memory. Galt — one is inescapably reminded of *Bleak House* — writes his novel not only in narrative and dialogue but in symbols, in terms of recurring motifs and continuing imagery that powerfully reinforce its moral significance — the law as an entangling web; the insistent Jacob-Esau motif; above all the pervasive, greedy ('grippy') commercial imagery that affects everyone, even the good and the innocent. Life is conceived in terms of downpayments ('erls') or bank bills or rents or cash at hand ('sooms of lying siller') and the Leddy can move in one sentence, with unconscious irony, from the imagery (from *The Book of Job*) of life as a weaver's shuttle to a grim jest on 'Death, Eternity, and Co., great wholesale merchants'.

The Entail is a novel of great dramatic power. It is also a work of great linguistic subtlety. In each of his recent books, Galt had silently increased the dialect element. His readers, evidently undisturbed, had responded with increased sales. Galt was rendered confident that in this, his major novel, he could go one step further and use the full resources of the west-country Scots in which he had for some months been deliberately immersing himself. He made *The Entail* a linguistic *tour-de-force*: characters and social levels are differentiated with great precision. The 'gentle' wife of the eldest son and the 'educated' third son speak current English; ministers and the numerous lawyers speak the upper-class Scots of their time; the full west-country rural dialect (rendered virtually in phonetic script) is reserved for Claud, Watty, and the Leddy — his most memorable characters. The novel is effective almost precisely to the degree to which he exploited the vernacular for which he had such a remarkable ear.

The initial sales of *The Entail* were steady, but unspectacular. Its power was recognized from its first appearance. But the new uncompromising use of dialect — its 'heathenish fault', as one of Galt's London friends called it — imposed limitations. Further, Galt's recently attracted band of enthusiastic readers had come to rely on him for enjoyable, 'pawky' Scots comedy. To them, the brutal and tragic story of *The Entail* came as a shock. The popular London weekly, the *Literary Gazette*, on 21 December voiced their dismay — 'The Walkinshaws of Grippy are a most unamiable and sordid race' — and went on to complain of the 'Clydesdale jargon' and the 'constant repetition of moral ugliness'. Other immediate reviews (e.g. that in the *Literary Chronicle*) were more appreciative of the novel's real quality, and by 13 January (1823) Galt was able to note with some satisfaction '*The Entail* comes on famously'; and Blackwood could report on 24 February 'Every body continues to speak highly of *The Entail*'.

It was soon apparent that his novel had found immediate favour with the main writers and critics of the day. Scott read it three times. 'Sir Walter's opinion . . . is very flattering indeed', Galt wrote Blackwood on 17 December, only a few days after the novel had been published. The Blessingtons lent a copy to Byron and Lady Blessington in her *Conversations of Lord Byron* recorded his confession that *The Entail* 'beguiled me of some portion of . . . tears, albeit unused to the melting mood';[3] the second edition of the novel cited Byron's further judgment; 'the portraiture of Leddy Grippy was perhaps the most complete and original that had been added to the female gallery since the days of Shakespeare'.[4] Coleridge's seal of approval has already been noted. Christopher North gave the book an enthusiastic review in the January 1823 number of the magazine — 'out of sight the best thing he has done'; and Jeffrey, in a major article on Galt in the October 1823 number of the *Edinburgh Review*, singled it out as 'a work undoubtedly of no ordinary merit'. Reputable

but modest sales were offset by the highest critical esteem.
The book continued to sell, though more slowly than Galt's
comic successes. The second edition did not appear till after
Galt's death. Its standing as his major work has never been in
doubt.

3

When Galt returned to London in December 1822, he had already
defected from Blackwood. The two men continued to exchange
letters till the following April. The tone of the correspondence
remains unchanged, without any hint of a breach, Blackwood
reporting on the progress of *The Entail*, Galt commenting on
Maga and on London gossip and on the forthcoming reprints of
The Ayrshire Legatees and *The Gathering of the West*. But before
he left Edinburgh, Galt had quietly offered his next novel to a
rival of Blackwood's, the long-established firm of printers turned
publishers, Oliver and Boyd, of Tweeddale Court in the High
Street of the Old Town.

Galt arrived back in London with the plans for his new novel
accepted and — as a bonus — a commission to write a critical
introduction for a new edition of Henry Mackenzie. The firm of
Oliver and Boyd still possesses some forty of Galt's letters,[5] written
between later 1822 and the end of 1824, and the very first of
these, sent by Galt on 17 December 1822 immediately on reach-
ing London, reported to George Boyd the progress of both projects. Within a couple of months Galt had so firmly committed
himself that he wrote Boyd on 24 February 1823 'I wish you
would try *quietly* to buy back from Blackwood the Annals of the
Parish and the Provost . . . I wish if possible to recover an interest
in it — You are perhaps aware that an arrangement of this kind
took place with the first series of the tales of my Landlord — I do
not however wish to be seen in the business'.

It was not a situation that could last. Blackwood suspected
nothing, though he was vaguely worried by Galt's unwonted in-
activity. On 24 February he was 'sadly vexed and disappointed'
at the non-arrival of promised articles for which he had held
space in the magazine. Has Galt, he wrote, been 'laid up'? Galt
was not laid up. He was briskly engaged in his 'public business'

and writing solidly for George Boyd. At the Easter Recess, he had
'five weeks leisure' from London and came north to Leith, writing Boyd on 15 March that he had come to 'finish the job' but
wished 'as long as possible to remain incognito and without going
to Edinburgh'. It is difficult to see how in the close-knit Edinburgh of the early nineteenth century he hoped to keep his
presence secret for more than a few hours, particularly when as
early as 10 April, he was making enquiries about renting a house,
Elie Lodge, for his family.[6]

In any case, Blackwood had proofs waiting for him — of the
second edition of *The Ayrshire Legatees* and of an issue in two
different formats of *The Gathering of the West*. Two days later,
on 17 March, Galt — at two miles distance from Blackwood —
sent a letter through the post, asking for his proofs, and saying
that he was 'much occupied'. Blackwood was — not unnaturally
— 'a good deal surprised' at this letter. Galt remained in his
Leith hotel, and returned the corrected proofs. He also sent in the
manuscript of a 'Letter from London' as the first of a new series
for Maga. Blackwood responded coldly on 1 April, forwarding
copies of the new editions; on the 'Letters' project he elected to
hedge — 'I have been so terribly plagued, after commencing a
series, by finding either that the author did not go on with it, or
did not continue in the way one expected'. Could Galt send a few
more Letters? He would pay at the rate of ten guineas a sheet for
'whatever of these are inserted in the Magazine'. He was, not
unreasonably, offended and hurt by Galt's secret arrival. Less
reasonably, he wrote what might have been a fair offer to a new
contributor. But to have it suggested — to a known, indefatigable,
and dependable contributor — that 'the author' could not complete a series once started, and that he might — or might not —
get his ten guineas was more than Galt could stomach. Fortified
by the knowledge that Oliver and Boyd had just paid him £100,
Galt strode up Leith Walk to 17 Princes Street.

What took place between the two angry men has not been
recorded in any study of Galt. There is no record in either of his
two autobiographical books. The record exists, however, in full
detail in some unpublished pages of the Blackwood Letter-Books.
Blackwood told the whole story to his Irish contributor, Dr
Maginn, in a letter of 23 April:

'You would be surprised at seeing by the Papers that Galt has gone to Oliver & Boyd with his new work. Perhaps it will be no great loss to me for I doubt he is not well fitted to give the unction which a work on the Covenanting side would require. He has behaved very ungratefully to me for he never even made me the offer or told me he had such a work in view, till he came down here a few weeks ago, and called on me, and informed me he had put it into other hands. We parted last year when he left this after finishing the Entail, on the best possible terms, and I had letters from him of the most friendly sort down almost to the day of his arriving here. The only reason or apology he offered for his conduct was that last year before he had finished the M.S. of the Entail, I told him he had been publishing so rapidly I would not wish him to bring out any other Book for nearly 12 months — This remark was called forth by his applying for £200 or £300 to account without his being able to say he had any particular Book in view though I have previously paid him in full (£525) for the copyright of the Entail. Nothing farther passed betwixt us at the time, and we had no quarrel of any kind. I have not yet had any quarrel with him, though I was obliged to tell him that his conduct had not been such as I thought I had reason to have expected. He is still here and comes to the shop as usual. My feelings however are quite changed though my external behaviour is not. The Prof. and L. think he has both behaved very ill to me and absurdly as to himself. Mrs B. is quite indignant at him as my Brother and his wife. He lived with them some months while he was writing Sir Andrew Wylie. He has never had the civility to call at their house or mine, — perhaps there is a virtuous feeling of shame in this. Well this is a strange world and one does not know whom to trust.'[7]

Maginn's reply from Cork made light of the matter — Galt, in his opinion was no great loss — 'It is probable that in a tradesman point of view you will lose little by not publishing "Ringan Gilhaize", for G. is writing too fast. Even Waverley himself is going it too strong on us, and he is a *leetle* better trump than Galt.' Blackwood's was not entirely a 'tradesman point of view'. He had his publisher's pride. But Galt had gone. Even in the magazine, where he had been almost a monthly event, his only certain appearances in the whole of 1823 total two, a political article, 'Bandana on the Abandonment of the Pitt System' in

May, and a lively narrative fragment, 'Sawney at Doncaster' in October. To these can possibly be added 'Scraps from London' in the June number, very likely pieced together from the 'Letter from London' he had offered in March. But these were, quite literally, merely scraps and fragments. His real work was going to Oliver and Boyd. The correspondence between Galt and Blackwood came to an abrupt stop. Apart from a few formal interchanges in the two following years, it was not to be resumed till Galt returned from Canada in 1825.

6. Galt in orbit

1

GALT'S FIRST novel for Oliver and Boyd broke new ground. In *Old Mortality* (1816), Scott's instinctive sympathy for a society based on law and order led him to portray the Scottish covenanters of the seventeenth century as religious fanatics and armed rebels, who met a deserved defeat at the Battle of Bothwell Brig. Galt had read the novel with dismay. Scott, he wrote in his *Literary Life*, 'treated the defenders of the Presbyterian Church with too much levity'. Some of Galt's own ancestors had been 'Cameronian' covenanters who had suffered in the campaign for conscience sake, and he must have read with some distaste Scott's dismissal (in chapter 33) of the fugitives from the battle as 'wild western whigs'. When Galt returned in 1822 to the same western country to write *The Entail*, he was shaping in his mind his next novel, *Ringan Gilhaize*, a Tale of the West, in defence of his dissenting forebears. The two books were so present at one time in his mind that a 'Ringan Gilhaise', the Leddy's cousin, makes a momentary appearance in *The Entail*. The farm of the Grippy he set deliberately near Bothwell Brig, which he came to see as the symbol of a covenanting conscience, dormant in Claud but not dead. The great climax, Claud's final and dramatic change of heart, is accomplished against 'a distant strain of wild and holy music', no mysterious off-stage chorus but 'Cameronians from Glasgow and the neighbouring villages' holding a commemorative service on the old battle-field. Already in *The Entail* Galt was busily envisaging his next novel.

Once he got the go-ahead from George Boyd, Galt set to work on the new novel with his usual despatch. On 19 December he asked Boyd for the loan of background books. On 6 January he told Lady Blessington he was 'all-heart engaged in my new novel

"The Scottish Martyre" '.[1] He sent Boyd 'half the first volume'
on 13 January and had completed this volume by the end of the
month. Manuscripts, a double set of proofs, and revises shuttled
between London and Edinburgh in February, and the second
volume was complete by 4 March. The third volume he wrote in
Edinburgh in late March and April. Oliver and Boyd were both
the printers and the publishers, and in early May appeared (in an
edition of 3000) *Ringan Gilhaize or The Covenanters By the
author of 'Annals of the Parish', 'Sir Andrew Wylie', 'The
Entail'* etc. The third volume concluded with an important
'Postscript by the Author', on his use of Scots.

Ringan Gilhaize is Galt's most carefully prepared book. He
visited the scenes he described; he knew every foot of the west
country, and Edinburgh had become familiar; his *Literary Life*
records a special visit he made to the site of the Battle of Killicrankie, where he salvaged abandoned weapons and armour and
'gathered traditions'. He had George Boyd send him parcels of
books on the period and made particular use of William Mait-
land's *History of Edinburgh* (1753) and Robert Wodrow's *History
of the Sufferings of the Church of Scotland* (1721). With a wry
reference to the 'heathenish fault' attributed to *The Entail*, he
told Boyd 'it shall not be too Scotch neither'. 'The style I have
chosen', he wrote to Lady Blessington, 'is that grave, cool, and in
some degree obselete, but emphatic manner which was employed
by the covenanting authors'.[2] Finally, as he records in his *Autobiography*, he gave much thought to the narrative technique.
Galt was in early 1823 too resentful to see the irony of the situation, but (consciously or unconsciously) he followed Blackwood's
previous advice on novel-writing to the letter, and wrote the entire
narrative in the first person and 'kept out of view every thing
that might recall the separate existence of the author'.

Ringan Gilhaize is the story of the two-century struggle of the
Scottish church for independence. The century of the Reformation
is retold in the first volume by Ringan from the memories of his
grandfather, agent and spy for the early reformers. In the later
volumes, Ringan emerges as the representative seventeenth-century
covenanter, undergoing in his single person all that had happened
to many, fighting every battle from Rullion Green to Bothwell
Brig and Killicrankie, suffering defeat, pursuit, imprisonment, and

the slaughter of his family, till he becomes the dedicated lone avenger of the dramatic final chapters, the 'chosen instrument' to summon the enemy Claverhouse (and here the commercial imagery of *The Entail* interposes) 'to the audit of his crimes'.

Perhaps because of his involvement with the theme and the hard work he had put into the preparation, *Ringan Gilhaize* always remained his favourite book. It did not impress the early reviewers. The *Literary Gazette* of 24 May accused Galt of mining 'as long as the material and the market lasts'. The *Monthly Magazine* of 1 June was respectful but unenthusiastic. Jeffrey, more fairly, in the October *Edinburgh Review* recognized that the work was written with 'labour and care', but 'still the book is tiresome, and without effect'. Oliver and Boyd had no reason to regret the £500 they paid for the copyright; two-thirds of the printing sold within a reasonable time. Many readers found in it what Allan Cunningham, in a letter to Galt of 6 June 1823, called the 'sharp features and homely beauties of living nature'.[3]

Technically, it presents some difficulties. The device of auto-biography — extended over 130 years by the narrative of the hero's grandfather — imposes a strain on credulity. Galt, close to his background reading, writes occasional long stretches of what in the persona of Ringan he candidly calls 'the public highway of history'. Yet, for all that, *Ringan Gilhaize* is an impressive book, a remarkable non-romantic historical novel that skilfully evokes the stresses of an earlier period, so realistically convincing in its authenticity that Galt (as with *Annals of the Parish*) had finally to insist that it *was* fiction. 'The sentiments which it breathes', he wrote in the *Literary Life*, 'are not mine, nor the austerity that it enforces, nor at all the colour of the piety with which the enthusiasm of the hero is tinged'. Galt, at heart a detached eighteenth-century man of the Enlightenment, had written what still remains the most sympathetic recreation in literature of the harshly independent, dour yet admirable spirit of Scottish calvinism, a considerable feat of creative imagination.

Galt remained with Oliver and Boyd during 1823 and 1824. From Constable he did receive a 'promise' of £250[4] for a volume in the *Miscellany* series on the life of William Paterson, the projector of the Darien Colony, and he later recorded that at the cost of 'much expense and research' he collected considerable material, but he could not find time to complete the book, and Oliver and Boyd (who paid him and did not merely promise money) remained his mainstay. It was a pacific relationship. George Boyd was, unlike Blackwood, an undemanding publisher. He confined himself in his letters to business details, made no suggestions, proposed no amendments, and simply printed what Galt provided. Galt, on his side, had learnt some caution and did not press undue demands — on *Ringan Gilhaize*, he wrote Boyd on 3 February 1823, 'if you . . . will make me an offer for the copyright I shall not be very *propugnacious* to deal with.' The advances he asked for, and received, were (on the evidence of the letters) modest — £100 on 24 March 1823 for *Ringan Gilhaize*, £50 on 19 September for *Wolsey*, and £100 on 14 October for *The Spaewife*.

The situation was made even easier by Galt's decision of Easter 1823, to move from London to Scotland. He had in the previous year become particularly intimate with Dr D. M. Moir, a physician of Musselburgh, near Edinburgh, who as 'Delta' (usually signed with the Greek letter 'Δ') was a frequent contributor to Maga. Galt had still plenty of negotiations to complete in London, but these were concentrated in the parliamentary session. His boys' education (with an old friend, Dr Valpy, who had a school in Reading) was proving expensive. In his *Autobiography* he made rather more drama of the decision than it probably was in reality — 'being sick of a life of adventure and having before me only the education of my children, I resolved to remain in the neighbourhood of Edinburgh'. He took a house in Eskgrove, close to Moir. His family moved in the late summer of 1823 for the opening of the school year; Galt, as he told Boyd, lodging 'pro tempore at the Salopian Coffeehouse Charing Cross', till he joined them in September.

By the close of the two-year period Oliver and Boyd had published a total of six works by Galt. As soon as he finished *Ringan Gilhaize* he began — characteristically — on two new projects: another Scottish historical novel and a collection of elegant extracts of prose and poetry which he proposed to call 'The Winter Visitors'. These, and the critical essay on Mackenzie, occupied the remaining months of 1823. There were some printing delays

— 'types being otherwise engaged' — but the historical novel, *The Spaewife A Tale of the Scottish Chronicles By the author of 'Annals of the Parish', 'Ringan Gilhaize' etc.* came out in three volumes (in an edition of 3000) in December; the collection of extracts (title and conception having undergone a radical alteration), appeared as *The Bachelor's Wife A Selection of Curious and Interesting Extracts with Cursory Observations By John Galt Esq.*, in a one-volume edition of 2000 in February, 1824. The works of Henry Mackenzie were in print by December 1823, prefaced by a *Critical Dissertation on the Tales by John Galt Esq.*, and were published early in the new year.

George Boyd was more than satisfied, and looking forward to a continuous flow of Galt books. On 19 September 1823, he contracted to publish a third edition of the 1812 *Wolsey*, of which Galt had retained the copyright. In response to Galt's enquiry 'As these bring all my present engagements to a close — what's next to be done?' he replied on 20 November 1823 'If you have fixed upon a subject for another novel you cannot do better than proceed . . . we are most anxious to act liberally towards you.' Galt was, inevitably, prepared to proceed not on one scheme but on several — another selection of elegant extracts (this time from books of travel); 'a little compilation from all my tales and entitled Views of Scottish Life and Manners'; a modern novel to be called 'The Housekeeper'. In the end, since London business required his continuous presence between February and August 1824, he settled on one — and quite different — project. It was *Rothelan*, yet another historical novel. He was still determined to keep up with Sir Walter.

In Eskgrove and later in London he wrote two volumes of the novel, and returned to Scotland in mid-August to write the third. But a hasty summons to his other life in the south, the growing demands of his 'public business', the strong possibility that it would culminate in a swift departure to Canada, led him to finish the story quickly — 'To provide against the worst', he wrote from London on 23 September, 'I have determined to complete *Rothelan* in the part I am now on'. Since novel readers of the time demanded their three volumes, virtually irrespective of content, Galt provided Boyd with the mandatory third volume, made up of three long romantic stories (under the general title of *The*

Quarantine or Tales of the Lazaretto) which he had submitted
unsuccessfully to Blackwood in 1822, one of them the tale that
Blackwood had indignantly rejected because it shocked his feelings. The patient Dr Moir in Musselburgh was landed with the
job of patching and editing four different sets of manuscript for
the printer — and then of proof-reading both *Wolsey* and
Rothelan.

Boyd accepted the situation with complete composure. The
third edition of *Wolsey* appeared in October in an edition of 750;
*Rothelan A Romance of the English Histories By the author of
'Annals of the Parish', 'Ringan Gilhaize', 'The Spaewife' etc.*, in
an edition of 2000 in November. It was dedicated to Lady Sarah
Robinson, the wife of the chancellor of the exchequer. Galt had
a copy bound 'in the *royal* manner' and presented to the King.
He saw his own first copy of *Rothelan* on 7 November and wrote
indignantly the next day that he had found an error in the third
volume and proposed to take action to 'suspend the publication'.
Oliver and Boyd's reply of 12 November (which could quite fairly
have been a remonstration at the burden imposed on Dr Moir) is
a masterpiece of crawling apology, concluding with the slyly
sensible comment that an injunction 'might hurt you as well as
us'. It was a letter worthy of Mr Pawkie. Galt recognized defeat,
and had the good grace to retract, laughing off his own letter as
'a quiz'.

With such an easy-going publisher, it should have been a great
opportunity. Galt was permitted to write as he pleased. There
was no pressure, no interference. The sad truth is that after
Ringan Gilhaize, which did have quality, his Oliver and Boyd
books are without value. *The Bachelor's Wife* is pure pot-boiler.
The two historical novels are not incompetently written. 'I read
the *Spaewife* of Galt', Scott entered in his *Journal*, 'There is
something good in it, and the language is occasionally very
forcible'.[5] Galt was too skilled a technician to write badly. The
fault of *The Spaewife* and *Rothelan* lies deeper. Writing on the
eighteenth century, which he knew and understood, he is sharp,
precise, in control. Writing on the sixteenth and seventeenth
centuries, his realistic historical sense deserts him and he is blindly
unaware that the genre he has chosen is fancy-dress fiction, sentimental and romantic evocation of history, intrinsically worthless.

The error is compounded by dialogue in the language of melo-
drama. 'I am undone' (says Sir Amias to his lady in *Rothelan*)
'my honour is ruined forever'. 'I do' (says the Countess of Atholl
to the Earl in *The Spaewife*) 'by our long cohabitation and faithful love, implore you not to embark on this business'. Galt, con-
ceivably, had been reading too much Henry Mackenzie.

For a man who had touches of near-genius, Galt had a quite
remarkable lack of self-critical ability. On many occasions he
acknowledged that he did not know when he was writing well
and when he was writing badly. George Boyd was no guide. He
simply printed what Galt sent in. The reading public of the time
was no guide. They bought as many copies of *The Spaewife* as of
Annals of the Parish; they bought many more copies of his later
money-spinner *Lawrie Todd* than of his masterpiece *The Entail*.
Had Galt moved in literary circles he might have come up against
real criticism; but he preferred the company of men (and women)
of fashion and of the world of affairs. 'How glad I would be',
Blackwood unburdened himself to Maginn, 'if Galt were always
to write what is worthy of himself'. What Galt really needed was
what he had lost, a publisher who would fight back.

Galt in Eskgrove in the later months of 1823 was instinctively
working round to accepting this. He was living only a few miles
from Blackwood's shop and he sent in some tentative peace-
offerings. Blackwood printed two of them in Maga, political
articles, 'Bandana on Representation' in January 1824, and
'Bandana on Emigration' in April. In mid-year Galt sent in
further articles from London. Blackwood remained cautious — on
7 August he feared 'the article on Shakespeare would not do', and
a sketch of Byron had arrived too late for the number, but 'I hope
you will be here soon when we will talk of all these matters'. He
was thawing, slowly. Galt offered him a fuller Byron article on
25 October — 'but you must promise to insert it'. Blackwood
complained on 29 October to Maginn that Galt 'feels a little sore
I daresay, as Authors never think the fault lies with them, but
with the stupid person who does not see the value of what is
offered to him'. The article, 'Lord Byron's Conversations', duly
made its appearance in the November Maga.

This stately and almost ritualistic *pas de deux* was clearly the
prelude to a reconciliation. It was broken off abruptly by Galt's

departure for Canada in the first few days of 1825. Galt did not return till June. One of his first acts was to invite Blackwood to dinner — 'let me know tomorrow when you will take a steak here, and come half an hour before dinner that we may have some conversation'. The quarrel was over. They could begin again on the old basis.

3

It is not the purpose of this study of Galt's literary career to follow in such documented detail his part in Canadian affairs. Galt kept him 'public business' and his literary activity in separate compartments. In private, he consistently preserved a distinction, which he took some trouble to ensure that the public should accept, between the 'John Galt, Esq.', who drafted memoranda for Ministers, and 'the Author of *Annals of the Parish*', who figured so prominently on his title-pages. As *The Spaewife* was due to be mentioned in the public journals, he wrote Boyd on 4 December 1823, 'I wish my name as little brought in as possible — You know my parliamentary concerns, and some folk are apt to think that business may be neglected by and for the vanities of authorship'. When he came later to recount the story of his life, he wrote it in two separate works, the *Autobiography* and the *Literary Life*, almost as if he were writing of two entirely different persons. To the 'public business' of Canada he gave much of his time and energy. His own account of his role fills close on three hundred pages of the *Autobiography*; and this has been supplemented in considerable fullness from public records and archives in a monograph published in 1920 by the Canadian scholar, R. K. Gordon.

Canada left a deep mark on what I have called Galt's 'other life'. Its impact on his writings was curiously unimportant. To his family, Canada brought the kind of success that Galt dreamed of: all three of his sons went there in early manhood and prospered in their new country; two of them attained high office and achieved knighthoods; after Galt's death in 1839, his widow joined her favourite Alick, the able youngest son, Alexander Tilloch Galt, and within two years could write to the solicitous Miss Pigott (who had been hinting at an application on her behalf to the Literary Fund) that she was living 'in the enjoyment of every comfort'.[6] Elizabeth Galt's reply was not Scottish pride. She was writing from the home of a future Minister of Finance. All this was too late for Galt. To him, involvement in Canada brought nothing but years of hard work, increasing frustration, and finally penury and disaster.

When America declared war on Britain in 1812 and moved troops over the Canadian border, many settlers in Upper Canada (now Ontario) suffered losses. For some years after the close of hostilities they looked, without success, to Britain for compensation. Galt first became involved in Canadian affairs when he was appointed in December 1820 (he called it an 'unexpected occurrence') agent for the claimants. His fee depended on his success, and he set to work with vigour. His negotiations with an unwilling Treasury, even with the assistance of friendly Members of Parliament like Edward Ellice, lasted over two years and it was not till March 1822 that the authorities agreed to sanction a public loan to meet the claims. The terms of the loan proved impracticable and Galt had to start again. During the ensuing two years, a further proposal for a loan on a different basis was negotiated, the interest charges to be borne equally by the British and the Canadian governments. This time it was the Canadian authorities who made difficulties. They recognized the settlers' plight; but refused to provide their own share of the interest.

Once again Galt had to make a fresh start. Looking around for another source of money, he drew on his now considerable knowledge of the Province, and proposed the sale of vast areas of its unexploited and uninhabited Crown Reserves. The Colonial Office showed interest and Galt was authorized to look for venture capital. Such was his influence and powers of persuasion among men of means in London that within a month he had gathered together a provisional committeee and a company was formed in July 1824. Galt was appointed secretary. The Colonial Office, however, made it clear that the expected revenue from sales would go to meet the civil expenses of the Province: His Majesty's Government would not countenance any use of these particular funds for the relief of Galt's claimants. Galt protested, without success. From time to time he continued to plead their cause; but the aggrieved settlers — for whom he had spent four years of

negotiations — simply faded from official view; and with them
vanished Galt's hope of being paid by them a fee for his services.
His energies forthwith were channelled into the new Canada
Company.

The Company was, in Galt's term, 'formed' in July 1824.
There was still much to be done. It was at this stage no more than
a group of private citizens with plans. Before it could operate as it
intended it had to acquire full legal personality by royal charter.
There still lay ahead two further years of protracted negotiation
with both British and Canadian authorities, separated by the
month-long passage of the Atlantic Ocean, before final agreements
could be signed. The charter was not granted till August 1826.
Meantime, in the later months of 1824, none of those directly
concerned had even seen the territory they proposed to buy and
sell. A board of five commissioners (one of whom was Galt) was
accordingly set up, and they took ship to examine and value the
lands. It was in these final months of consultation and pressure
before departure that Galt hurried his *Rothelan* to its abrupt
conclusion. The commissioners sailed in January 1825, and spent
March and April 1825 in Upper Canada, moving around, hearing evidence on valuations, examining charts of the territories.
They signed their report on 2 May and were back in Liverpool
on 5 June. Everything then paused while the Colonial Office
slowly brooded on their findings. Galt went to Eskgrove to see his
family. He was back in London by early July, standing by in case
he was required, living in apartments provided at Canada House,
St Helen's Place, by the Company. He had time on his hands and
he picked up his pen and began to write again.

4

Blackwood happened at the time to be in London. He sent round
as an appropriate gift to a returned Atlantic traveller a three-
volume work he had just published, *Brother Jonathan* by John
Neal, an American contributor to Maga. Galt's reply to this
friendly gesture was to invite him to dinner and discussion at his
Canada House apartment — 'I want to speak to you about three
of my dormant plans, and it may depend on yourself whether you
will have anything to do with them before I speak to any other —

I say this the more frankly because I perceive by a return from Oliver and Boyd's [London] correspondents . . . that I may be brought into a new negotiation'. The following month he asked Oliver and Boyd in Edinburgh for a report on his sales, and they provided the same day (18 August) a meticulously careful analysis of printings and sales (see Appendix 2).

Although this showed his total sales were approaching a gratifying 9000, Galt had already settled to return to Blackwood.

He had plenty of time for writing. Government activity was at a standstill during the summer, and Galt was back in Eskgrove by August, and not recalled to London till December. He had, one might have imagined, much of interest to write, arising from his Canadian trip. Nothing was further from his mind. Canada to him was business, not the stuff of literature. He began on two of his three 'dormant plans'. In September Maga announced that *The Omen* was 'in the press' and on 11 September Galt told Blackwood 'I think you may announce *The Last of the Lairds* or the life and opinions of Malachi Mailings Esq. of Auldbiggings'. The October Maga carried a full-page displayed advertisement for both. It must have seemed to Blackwood like the fecund days of 1822 all over again, and, although Galt's letter made it clear that the second book was only in the planning stage, Maga boldly (and mendaciously) advertised it as 'in the press and speedily will be published'. Blackwood admitted him once again to his inner circle, commissioning his now reunited team — Maginn, Christopher North and Galt — to write a swaggering thirty-three page Preface with which Maga would open the new year in the issue of January 1826. Galt in addition, had a brief contribution on Byron in the October Maga and wrote a review 'Moore's Life of Sheridan' which appeared the following February. He was firmly back in favour.

In Eskgrove, Galt had time to enjoy his family. This is an aspect of his life which never appears in his works. His personal life (like his other lives) was tightly compartmented. It was his affair, and he saw no reason to make a public show of it even in his autobiographical books. The surviving private family letters give glimpses of a normal and happy group: Galt writing to the boys about their pony; to his wife on the progress of his mission; she of a Bible which she is buying for Alick; of a cheque she has received; she invites guests to dinner; the boys in Eskgrove write their regular Sunday letter to their father in London. Galt fretted at the long absences that his business interests enforced, but (the son of a merchant skipper) accepted them as inescapable.

While he was in Scotland this year he made two family trips to the west of Scotland. The first was to his birthplace, Irvine, with his mother and sister on 7 September, when he was astonished and delighted to receive the freedom of that Royal Burgh. He was even more astonished (and delighted) at the 'venerable' old man who made the presentation speech in broad dialect — no other than 'Provost Pawkie' in person; Galt's original (Bailie Fullarton) was — contrary to Galt's belief — still very much alive. The second trip, to Greenock, in early December, was sadder; his mother was ill and unlikely to recover. It was the one shadow on what had been a pleasant and busy four months, reunited both with his family and with his publisher. They came to an end when the Company and Wilmot-Horton, the under-secretary of state for the Colonies, beckoned him south. He was in London by 20 December and was to remain there for most of the ensuing year.

The first to be published of the books advertised in October was *The Omen*, which was being printed in London in the latter part of the year. The title-page dates the book 1825; however there were delays — 'the holidays have interrupted the printing', Galt wrote on 3 January — and it did not appear till February 1826. The book was without indication of authorship. Even the usual 'Author of *Annals of the Parish*' was withdrawn. Galt was prepared to venture on a double-blind test of his ability to attract readers. The first copies arrived in Edinburgh by coach, and the following day (20 February) Blackwood wrote that the Professor 'has been prodigiously struck by it and quite puzzled as to the Author'. Scott read the book as soon as it appeared and entered in his *Journal* 'Read a little volume called *The Omen* — very well written — deep and powerful language. *Aut Erasmus aut Diabolus*, it is Lockhart or I am strangely deceived'.[7] On 25 February the *Literary Gazette*, which had been complaining of Galt for some years, gave it a long and respectful review, suspecting in *its* turn the author to be Scott. Galt's ruse had certainly been successful.

The Omen is a short horror tale of novella length. A melancholic youth, brought up in ignorance of his origins, grows from childhood to manhood, receiving from time to time mysterious intimations of some dread secret in his parentage. He inherits wealth, travels, falls in love. The catastrophe comes at his wedding, when he at the last moment is prevented from marrying his own sister. Galt handles this tale of suspense, with its menacing atmosphere and its terror scenery, with some skill, in a genre and language so different from his Scots novels that it is no wonder his contemporaries looked elsewhere for the author. Scott re-read the tale when he agreed to write a review for the July number of Maga. On the second reading, he was less pleased with the management of the plot but on the whole book he confirmed his earlier judgment — 'there is something in the work which pleases me, and the style is good'.[8] Once again the first to appreciate Galt's achievement were his fellow processionals.

During the year, Galt had three articles published in Maga, 'Private Poetry' in May (a review of a poetical 'rhapsody' published anonymously by his friend, Lord Blessington), and two political articles, 'Bandana on Colonial Undertakings' in August and — expansion of his 1824 article with the same title — 'Bandana on Emigration' in September, both of them propaganda pieces supporting the current plans of the Canada Company. Elated by his recent success in terror-fiction, he wrote in March part of a short story 'full of mysticism and poetry' called '666 or the Number of the Heart' but though Blackwood had it set up in type and forwarded proofs, Galt (unusually for him) left it unfinished and returned to his main literary preoccupation, *The Last of the Lairds*, begun the previous year at Eskgrove. A small section of it had already appeared, entitled, 'A Feeling Neighbour. A fragment', in January 1826 in a collection of prose and poetry *The Literary Souvenir*, an 'annual' edited by Alaric Watts.

5

The writing and re-writing of *The Last of the Lairds* extended over more than a year. For Galt, as the Company's long negotiations came each month closer to success and there seemed every

chance that he would spend several years of his life in Canada as
a high official of the Company, the novel came to have a special
significance. It was not just the story of the last of the lairds, of
(as he wrote Blackwood on 23 August) 'the actual manners which
about 25 years ago did belong to a class of persons and their
compeers in Scotland — the west of it — but who are now ex-
tinct'. It was to be his final Tale of the West. Galt's allowance as
secretary of the Company had been set at £1000 a year. If he
went to Canada as the Company's senior official, his future was
secure. He could afford to abandon 'the vanities of authorship';
The Last of the Lairds was his farewell to novel-writing.

Galt put more thought into *The Last of the Lairds* than into
any of his other books, with the possible exception of *Ringan
Gilhaize*. Its progress and development can also be documented
more fully than anything he wrote, since its composition was the
topic of a constant exchange of letters between Edinburgh and
London extending over many months. Blackwood soon began to
'interfere'. Galt on this occasion defended himself and his method
of writing a novel with mounting vigour. Secure in his thousand-
a-year secretaryship, he could afford to fight back. A total of
twenty-six letters was to be written before the contestants gave up,
unconvinced, their patience — and Galt's time in England —
finally exhausted.

The central theme of *The Last of the Lairds* had been fore-
shadowed five years earlier in the last chapter of *Sir Andrew
Wylie*, where Miss Mizy 'in sorting some old papers had made a
great literary discovery', a manuscript volume written by the
laird, her dead brother, which contained 'a most full account of
all manner of particularities anent the decay of the ancient
families of the west country'. When Galt in late 1825 set himself
to the long-promised novel, he began writing it in the form of the
dead laird's journal. But he soon came to see that this imposed
self-defeating limitations. The reminiscences, subtle and varied, of
the astute Mr Pawkie could be deployed over an entire book;
those of Malachi Mailings, whom he envisaged as a silly old man,
could not. 'There is something in imbecility', he explained to
Moir as the book neared its conclusion, 'that will not suffer it to
endure much handling'.[9]

Galt struggled for some months to find a technique for telling

his story, and by March 1826 had consigned two successive
versions to the fire, before he hit on the structure of an inner and
an outer narrative, the laird's reminiscences set within an outer
'authorial' framework. By such a device he achieved perspective
both on the laird himself and on the other characters in the book.
He could move at will from the small world of particularities of
the west country seen through the eyes (and in the Scots language)
of the laird to the particularities of the laird as seen through the
eyes of others. The mechanics inevitably involved his 'author' in
some implausible activity — copying out the laird's manuscript,
inadvertently eavesdropping at conversations, moving around to
meet people and record what he had heard. It is no more implausible than the similar narrator device in *Wuthering Heights*.

The novel is a dramatic and high-spirited farce, a return to the
Scottish comedy of his earlier triumphs. The improvident and
foolish old laird, his estate of Auldbiggings mortgaged to Mr
Rupees the local nabob, is persuaded with difficulty by the
'author' and the busybody Mrs Soorocks to save himself by a
reluctant marriage with one of the pair of elderly spinsters of
Barenbraes. The successive steps in the intrigue are presented in a
series of interlocking comedy scenes, culminating in an uproarious
Scottish wedding by declaration. Once married, the ill-assorted
pair combine forces to outwit the nabob. An impending parliamentary election discloses that, though Auldbiggings is mortgaged,
its franchise (or 'superiority') is a valuable asset that can be disposed of separately. The laird, with the shrewd assistance of his
new wife, conducts a riotous auction ('roup') and retires comfortably to Edinburgh on the proceeds — to write his memoirs for
Blackwood.

While the novel was being written, battle raged between author
and publisher. The early chapters were sent to Edinburgh and
Blackwood returned them promptly in proof — 'they are most
singular and original'; but were not some of the incidents 'perhaps a little strong'? Galt answered this charge by return post —
if a character had 'coarseness' an author must be course — 'if
there is any merit in any of my sketches it is in the truth of the
metaphysical anatomy of the characters, which though at first
felt as faults in the author, and thought coarse, I have seen in the
end been seen in their true light'. Blackwood retreated; found the

next set of chapters 'capital'; and remained satisfied so long as
Galt continued to develop the comedy scenes involving the laird.
By August, when Galt was expanding his gallery of characters, he
incautiously mentioned that 'the bringing out of the nabob's
character has led me to change the structure of the story'. Blackwood pounced — Galt, he wrote accusingly, should not write
'without having your plan definitively fixed'. 'The chapters
about the Nabob and Mrs Sourocks etc. though very good indeed
do not much advance the story. . . . The Laird, the Laird himself,
is what one wishes to see you giving in all his glorious originality
and peculiarity.' He concluded the letter by saying what he really
meant by all this — 'The Laird must not only be a good book, it
must be a first sale one'.

Galt's reply was the angry letter of 23 August, referred to in
earlier chapters, in which he recalled one by one every instance of
Blackwood's interference since 1821. 'Nobody', he bluntly
stated, 'can help an author with the conception of a character nor
in the evolution of a story. . . . I cannot proceed if I am interfered
with. . . . It does *not* come of arrogance, but from having confidence in myself'.[10] Blackwood first attempted a soothing reply —
he has 'thrown off 3000 copies'. A few days later on 6 September
he was able, since Galt had inadvertently allowed him a glimpse
into his workshop, to return to the attack: Galt has changed 'the
structure of the story' by abandoning 'so much of your original
and *admirable* hero, the Laird'. The controversy raged throughout September, the letters increasing in length and acerbity — 'if
a man has corns', Galt wrote, 'an accidental tread may be as
painful as a malicious stamp'. Blackwood reduced his planned
impression from 3000 to 2000; Galt found this 'ominous'. But
Blackwood persisted with his objections; and he finally turned the
whole set of proofs over to Moir, in the hope that the friendly
doctor could induce Galt to re-write the book.

Galt was at the end of his tether. The light, farcical — even
bawdy — comedy had been his safety-valve in what had been a
year of considerable stress. A multiplicity of conflicting and com-
peting interests had so frustrated the Company's plans that when
Galt's mother died in Greenock in July he was unable to leave
London to comfort his sister. He was living alone, except for a
servant, in the Company's apartment, and missed his family —

one of his many letters of this time to the under-secretary for the Colonies complained of 'the domestic privations which I have been obliged to endure'. Now his publisher was proving stubborn and throwing further difficulties in his way. In September he decided to pay a visit to Edinburgh, to see his family, and to convince Blackwood in person. But the Company, having at last received its charter, suddenly ordered Galt to proceed immediately to take charge of the selection of land in Upper Canada. Galt sailed in the first week of October, without the chance of seeing either his publisher or his family.

So far as he was concerned, in the last rushed days of preparation for departure, *The Last of the Lairds* had seen the last of John Galt. It was finished; Blackwood could do as he liked. 'You are fonder of controversy than I am', he wrote on 3 October, 'and I have no objection to your having the last word'. A few days later he sailed. His last action on the book was to write a long letter on 1 October to Moir, who had been gently trying to mediate: Galt set out in detail what he had been planning to achieve in the novel and left any final revision to Moir — 'With regard to those blemishes to which you advert do with them as you think fit: I give you full liberty to act; carve and change as you please'. Galt was off on a new career, authorship abandoned. *The Last of the Lairds* was, in the most literal sense, out of his hands.

The Last of the Lairds or The Life and Opinions of Malachi Mailings, Esq. of Auldbiggings. By the Author of Annals of the Parish, The Entail, etc. came out in November 1826. Galt wrote Moir the following year on 22 February from Quebec, where he had ultimately procured a copy, and — seeing for the first time what had been done with his story — expressed his 'very great obligations'. In the light of what had been done to his book, it is difficult not to feel that Galt's irony was once more at play.

Galt's letters to Moir, selected parts of which are printed in the *Memoir*, confirm that alterations had been made. Later readers of Moir's account could with some reason assume that he had simply tidied up Galt's copy for the printer by the removal of minor clerical 'blemishes'. Without the actual papers prepared for the printer, it was not possible to determine the extent or the nature of the alterations, and all later editions of *The Last of the*

Lairds have perforce been straight reprints of the edition of 1826. Fortunately, the copy for the printer has in recent years emerged. After remaining with the Moir family for close on a century and a half, it was in 1961 presented to the National Library of Scotland.

An examination of this remarkable document,[11] written in the handwriting of both men, reveals the full extent of Moir's interpretation of Galt's invitation to 'carve and change as you please'. Moir did not just 'edit', by removing clerical 'blemishes'. Considering the book full of 'vulgarity and uncleanness', he re-wrote almost every page, toning down consistently what Blackwood called 'strong', altering the dialect, inventing fresh incidents (some of them of considerable length), expunging offending words and phrases. He inserted a gratuitous and inappropriate reference to *The Omen*, and added over-written and sentimental passages never conceived by Galt and out of keeping with the context. He deleted the obstetrical incident in chapter iii ('whamling the young one into the world') that Blackwood had objected to; he eliminated a drunken riot (a 'stramash' of Paisley weavers who had 'gotten themselves fou') in chapter xxiv. In chapter xxxv the elderly Laird and his elderly new wife are despatched, in Galt's manuscript, with the injunction 'Ye'll gang intil Embro and live comfortable, like tua patriarchs, begetting sons and dochters, if ye can.' Moir's censorious pen firmly deleted the last seven words.

The conclusion of the book as published was entirely by Moir. Galt's manuscript had brought the novel to an end at chapter xxxvii. Moir dropped seven lines from the end of this chapter. He invented a new chapter xxxviii, working it up from a comic story provided by Blackwood. A new chapter xxxix followed, in which he married off the servants, Jock and Jenny Clatterpans — the only alteration to meet with Galt's approval. To conclude the book he salvaged the seven lines he deleted from the end of Galt's original story and expanded them to a full final chapter xl. It is not claiming too much to say that the lively, vigorous, and earthy *The Last of the Lairds*, as conceived and written by Galt, has never been printed. It awaits an editor more conscientious than Moir. Blackwood certainly had the last word.

In his later years, when he came to write his *Literary Life*, Galt said of *The Last of the Lairds* 'I meant it to belong to that series of fictions of manners, of which the Annals of the Parish is the beginning' but the published version, he wrote, had 'lost that appearance of truth and nature' which he intended. Writing his literary life in 1834 he claimed — diplomatically perhaps — that he could 'no longer remember' why the alterations were made. In 1826 he certainly knew and had protested continuously to Blackwood. But by the time the book came ultimately into his hands in distant Quebec and he saw what had been done, he was not prepared to battle. Early in 1827 he read the pallid shadow of his concluding *Tale of the West*. He contented himself with a politic letter of thanks to Moir. That part of his life, the days of novel-writing, was over. It may be accidental, but it is curiously significant, that the copy he read was not even his own. It had been lent to him by Lady Dalhousie, the wife of the Canadian Governor-General. Galt was once again the man of affairs, and a new life lay ahead of him in Canada.

7. The treadmill

1

AFTER LONG negotiations, the government had finally assigned the Canada Company a million acres of forest-land in Upper Canada (i.e. Ontario) stretching south from Lake Huron towards Lake Ontario. With a capital of £1,000,000, and the purchase-money of £145,000 payable over sixteen years, the Company could look forward to considerable profits. Meanwhile, the Huron Tract had to be surveyed, developed, sold, and settled. Galt's initial duties were to investigate and report. Within a few months he was put in charge, at a salary of £1600, as superintendent of the whole operation and began two busy years of varied and complex activity. He always remembered 1827 as 'the most active year of my whole life'. He travelled widely: to Quebec, to arrange matters with the government of Lower Canada; by canal and steam-boat to New York, to study land-tenure; by land and water round the million acres of the Huron Tract. He supervised the building of roads and the felling of forests, the establishment of a warehouse for company stores, the sale (for cash, kind, or labour) of land to settlers, the payment of the annual instalment due to the Provincial government, and the foundation of what soon became the towns of Guelph and Goderich. His old dream of power, of controlling a vast business enterprise, was at last coming true.

All this was intensely satisfying — 'I did not feel myself entering seriously the arena of life till I undertook my second mission to Canada' was how he opened his long account in the *Autobiography*. The pleasure was increased when his family joined him in the spring of 1828, the boys going to school in the longer established Lower Canada, while Galt and his wife set up house in Upper Canada in the new town of Guelph, in a house built of

85

logs but (as he wrote Moir) 'not without some pretensions to elegance'. It should have been, with all his hard work, the prelude to a second career of real distinction.

In fact, it was a prelude to disaster. Galt was simply not the man for the job. In spite of his energy, his organizing ability, his prompt and accurate on-the-spot decisions on what had to be done in a pioneering society, his financial probity, his clear-sighted prescience of the future Ontario's magnificent resources, the Canadian mission was for him (though not for Canada nor for the Company) a failure. Private and public documents and printed papers of the time offer many accounts of Galt during these two years. They exhibit two sharply contrasting views. The great majority write in terms of the highest praise — 'an upright and honourable gentleman' . . . 'Mr Galt's agency has been conducted with sound judgment' . . . 'he has laid a solid foundation for future profits' . . . 'Galt, whose character for probity and fair dealing was unimpeachable' . . . 'We, the undersigned inhabitants of the town and township of Guelph . . . request you to thank the Canada Company for all the benefits they have conferred on us, and the greatest of these we consider their having set you among us'.[1] Galt had his friends and admirers, and they were in the majority.

He had less success with the upper reaches of the hierarchical colonial society in which he had to operate. He proved himself something of a nuisance to the government authorities of Lower Canada, who regarded him as a 'politician', still pressing on them the 1820 settlers' claims which they wished to forget. The Lieutenant-Governor of Upper Canada suspected Galt (a life-long Tory) of radical tendencies and an inclination to meddle in politics. He reported unfavourably to London. Lord Byron had pointed out in the old days that Galt 'had not deference enough';[2] and in Canada he remained the same, too fond of persistently arguing with his political masters. To measure up to the demands of his position as superintendent he had to be all that he was, and in addition tactful and diplomatic. He was no diplomat. The straight-forward and blunt-speaking Galt was no Sir Andrew Wylie.

It was the minority — but official — view that crossed the Atlantic slowly in despatches to London and ultimately came to the ears of the directors of the Canada Company. They had their other worries concerning the activities of their distant and independent-minded superintendent. He reported monthly in some detail, and as business men they could not but see that funds were being disbursed freely — on roads, buildings, store-houses, barracks for immigrants, salaries, the costs of travel and surveys, even (they noted grimly) on the relief of destitute settlers. There was no hint yet of any return on their money. This, for what was in its nature a long-term investment, was not in itself of any immediate consequence. But when in 1828 public confidence in the Company's affairs waned, and its stock began to sell on the market at a discount, the directors — alarmed at something much more serious, an erosion of their capital — decided to send out a Mr Thomas Smith ostensibly as 'accountant and cashier' to have a look at what was going on. Galt at first was pleased — he needed a good clerk — but when he found that Mr Smith's salary was 'greatly beyond an adequate payment for the duties to be performed' he became suspicious, and was not greatly surprised to find his cashier was sending reports direct to London; nor to hear one morning in November 1828 that he had silently departed for England.

Galt did not stand a chance. The *Autobiography* describes his settlement of Guelph (in language that would have confirmed the worst fears of the Lieutenant-Governor) as 'an asylum for the exiles of so-called society — a refuge for the fleers from the old world and its systems fore-doomed'. Indeed he had privately by-passed the Lieutenant-Governor and on 21/22 June had provided Lord Dalhousie with an 'Outline of a plan for a new Colony' — with himself in the 'chief management' at a proposed £2000 a year. Dalhousie's reply was a diplomatic but friendly refusal.[3] What Galt was planning was a Wakefieldian colony, with himself as architect-in-chief. What the directors wanted was a reasonably prompt return on their money and their capital intact. As individuals they were friends of Galt. But business was business, and they decided to replace him. Accordingly, the bank in York, the capital of Upper Canada, was instructed not to meet Galt's drafts. It seems a drastic step, but in those days of slow communications it was probably the only effective way of ensuring that no further expenditure would be incurred. For Galt it was a public rebuke. He was sure that if he could get to England he could satisfy the directors; and — totally unaware that his usefulness to the Company was at an end — he left his family in Upper Canada and travelled overland to New York to take ship for Liverpool. Before he went on board the consul met him with his latest despatch — 'I was superseded by another gentleman'. The dream of power was finished.

Galt landed in Liverpool on 20 May 1829. The issue of 23 May of the *Edinburgh Literary Gazette* greeted him with a long appreciative essay, 'Literary Life of John Galt., Esq.', unsigned but written by Moir. Galt on arrival went immediately to London to see those directors with whom he was particularly close; his old friend, the Hon. Robert Downie, M.P. (to whom he had dedicated *The Provost*), assured him the recall was only temporary. But the Canada Company was itself fighting for survival and when the court of directors met on 12 June they were interested only in Galt's accounts, fastening in particular on one overexpenditure of £700 in an item of £4000. For a company capitalized at a million it seems slight; but the court's examination of Galt's accounts was only a routine formality. The directors had decided to cut their expenditure till better times should come, and Galt was part of their retrenchment. He had already been superseded as superintendent. There was no explicit dismissal from the Company's service; but there was no offer of further employment. Moir made a valiant attempt to put the case for Galt in the June issue of the *Edinburgh Literary Gazette*, reprinting in full a series of Canadian tributes to his integrity and good management, and attacking the 'mercenary gentlemen' who had disposed of Galt because 'he was not fast enough in wringing money from the settlement'. The gentlemen elected to preserve a discreet silence.

This down-turn in Galt's fortunes was the prelude to complete disaster. The low state of the Company's stock was already well known; Galt's virtual dismissal rapidly became public. When Galt left England in 1826, he owed various sums to a total of some £1100. While he was in Canada, in a well-paid position, his creditors had been happy to wait. Now that he had lost his job, they decided that it was time to get what they could and closed in on him. Had they come singly and at intervals, Galt could have contrived with the help of his friends to pay them off. But a series of simultaneous demands made this impossible. One of his creditors, Dr Valpy (to whom he still owed £197.14.0 for school fees and accrued interest), took legal action to recover the debt. Galt was unable to meet the demand. He was arrested for debt and on 15 July was committed to the debtors' prison of the King's Bench.

Galt, sharing with the Micawbers of his day the gloomy confines of the King's Bench, could hardly believe that a friend of such long standing could be so implacable; the simple truth is that the Reverend Richard Valpy, D.D. had insufficient understanding of the consequences of recourse to the law to foresee that his action would put his old friend in prison. He had been short of ready money himself at the time and (as he later recounted in the *Literary Gazette* of 21 September 1833) was 'induced, under what has since turned out to be erroneous advice, to act in a manner he would not have done if left to the dictates of his own head and heart . . . when the law is called in, the original parties have but little influence on the subsequent course and decision'. The legal process of the time for the recovery of debt, once started, was irreversible, and Galt, in his own words, 'retired from the arena of business with the sullenness of a vanquished bull'.

The penalty of the period was harsh. Galt later in his *Autobiography* recounts the incident in tones of injured innocence. His letters of the time make it clear he was not entirely blameless. In spite of all his pretensions to being a business man, he was not particularly effective in the conduct of his own affairs. There had been an occasional time in his life when money had been tight, but he had never been a poor man. He should, by now, have been tolerably well-off. Being compelled, in his circumstances, to render an account of his finances, he found (as he wrote Blackwood on 6 August) that his income over the previous ten years from all sources — fees, salaries, commissions, the annuity of £300, literary earnings and the rest — had averaged just under £2000 a year; and he had farms in Canada worth £2000. But he had (alas) fancied himself as a financier — 'had I not meddled with shares and Discounted Bills I should have at this time had £9000'. At least his family were secure in Canada. He had to make an assignment of his property in England and he remained confined till his discharge, on 10 November, under the Insolvent Act.

2

There was nothing for it but to turn once again to his pen. During his two years in Canada he had little time or inclination for publication. He had kept a rough journal, made some notes for possible stories with a Canadian setting, and twice had dashed off scripts ('The Visitors, or A Trip to Quebec' and 'An Aunt in Virginia') for amateur dramatic performances. He had accumulated (as he wrote Moir on 4 July 1829) 'a great mass of book-materials — the fruits of my solitary noctes in the Canadian wayside Taverns'. Towards the end of his stay in Canada he had written Blackwood in November 1828 that he was working on a series of London sketches, and Maga with superlative optimism announced in February 1829 that 'the Author of "Annals of the Parish", "Sir Andrew Wylie", etc. has just finished a New Work, under the title of "MY LANDLADY AND HER LODGERS". The MS. is expected by the first ship from New York, and the Work will be published without delay'. When Galt arrived in England, knowing full well it was not finished, he told Blackwood the MS still had to be copied. Blackwood responded on 1 June with his old enthusiasm — 'send me the MS. as it is by post Coach' — and enclosed a note for £50 to account. This shamed Galt into providing on 30 June four chapters, with the suggestion they might be published 'in "the Magazine" as "the Ayrshire Legatees" was done'. Blackwood on 21 July (unaware of the disaster that had meantime overtaken his author) was 'perfectly delighted', and 'My Landlady and her Lodgers' was given the place of honour as the 'opening article' of the August number of Maga.

When Blackwood heard in a few days' time of Galt's plight he rallied round in the most practical way. He could not get Galt out of debtor's prison, but he could provide him with regular income. On 30 July he told Galt to send Maga all he could: articles on Canada, more of 'My Landlady and her Lodgers', general articles, and 'as many as you can of your Anecdotes'. Galt set to work, and by next month Blackwood was delighted to have on hand 'a large supply of capital articles'. Since payments made out openly to Galt might fall into the hands of creditors, Blackwood astutely paid him on at least one occasion (28 October) with a draft made out to J. . . . . .T, leaving Galt to fill in the missing letters, and continued — 'You may rest assured I will not be slack in my remittances if you set yourself fairly and determinedly to do your best'.

With such practical friendship, Galt did indeed work determinedly. Seven out of the eight numbers of Maga published from August 1829 to March 1830 contain articles by Galt under a variety of *noms-de-plume*: 'Colonial Discontent; Part I Lower Canada; Part II Upper Canada' (signed 'CABOT') in September drew on his recent experiences. 'The Idiot, An Anecdote' (signed 'DOMENICHINO') in October, 'Tom Paine' (signed 'G.T.') in November, 'The Fate of the Caliph Motasser: Astrolab, or the Soothsayer of Bagdad' (unsigned) in February 1830, and 'The Spectre Ship of Salem' (signed 'NANTUCKET') in March 1830 fall under Blackwood's classification of 'anecdotes'. Galt's interest in economics (which he had earlier shown in his 'Bandana' articles) produced 'Thoughts on the Times' (signed 'AGRICOLA') in October and 'The Colonial Question' (signed 'AGRICOLA') in March 1830. Once he was free from the King's Bench he began a series on the London townscape and Maga published the first of these, 'On the Recent Architectural Improvements of London' (unsigned), in January 1830.

While these articles were appearing, Galt prepared, for the September, October and November numbers of Maga, three further instalments of 'My Landlady and her Lodgers'. It is no wonder that this work aroused Blackwood's enthusiasm, since it represented a return to the Scots humour and successful 'clishmaclaver' manner of *The Ayrshire Legatees*. The narrator is a young man of business who arrives (as Galt did) in London in 1804 to make his way in the world. He lodges with Mrs Winsom, a Scottish landlady, and she regales him with reminiscences of her lodgers. Within this simple framework, Galt contrives a series of tales lively and pathetic, all told in the dialect of which he was a master, and neatly set against the day-by-day life of London. It was a mixture calculated to attract readers on both sides of the Border. Four numbers proved enough to exhaust the vein. Galt, for once, did not need Blackwood's caution of 28 October that the last instalment 'I fear will not be thought as good as usual'. He had already decided the series was complete, writing

on 30 October 'The Landlady vexes me — I shall send no
more'.

All this was done while Galt was a prisoner in the King's
Bench. A fellow-contributor to Maga, R. P. Gillies, was in London at the time and his later *Memoirs of a Literary Veteran*
(1851) describes Galt working 'in *dour* silence and with imper-
turbable stoicism' at his writing. Galt was confined, but not
incarcerated. The King's Bench prison, in the Borough of South-
wark, was the least restrictive of the London debtors' prisons. It
had over two hundred rooms, a spacious courtyard with a market,
and inmates were free to roam those surrounding streets which
fell within the traditional 'rules' or liberties. Galt was able in
many ways to conduct a normal kind of life, writing as he cared,
sending and receiving letters and parcels, even (so long as his
creditors did not find out) receiving payments. He had his mail
delivered to the nearby Herbert's Coffee House, which was within
the 'rules'. It was humiliating, but it was not in any modern sense
'prison', and Galt soldiered on.

Cut off from his friends and his family and any possibility of
'business', he had plenty of time to write. The mass of work he
did for Blackwood was not even the major part of his output from
the King's Bench. While he was in Canada the firm of Hullett
Bros. and Co. had paid a premium on his life insurance. The
repayment of this Galt considered a first priority, and he met it
by closing at once with an offer of an immediate advance of £300
from the London publishers, Colburn and Bentley, on account of
a novel. Knowing that Colburn's shameless advertising methods
offended — and alarmed — the more sober publishers (who called
him 'the prince of puffers') Galt explained his action apologetically to Blackwood on 26 July — 'This affair I therefore trust
you will consider a business transaction and not affecting our
friendship'. Blackwood (30 July) was sorry that Galt had to go to
his rival Colburn ('Don Puffando') but agreed Galt had little
option. Galt stolidly set himself down to write a three volume
novel, *Lawrie Todd*, and completed it by the end of September.

Faced with the task of writing a novel quickly for a new publisher, Galt fell back on his recent experiences. Among the papers
which he had brought to England was a short manuscript autobiography of a Grant Thorburn, a successful New York merchant.

Using this as a starting point, he constructed the story of Lawrie Todd, an emigrant Scot who sets up a general store in the Canadian bush and thrives in the new settlement. Lawrie Todd was a kind of low-key Sir Andrew Wylie ('tod' in Scots is the wily fox) and much of his experiences were Galt's own. *Lawrie Todd or The Settlers in the Woods by John Galt* was published in January 1830. For the first time (and for his own reasons) Galt put his name on the title-page of the novel. In the preface Galt suggested that though the novel was primarily for the reader's entertainment it could be 'useful to the emigrant'. The photographic realism of his picture of colonial life appealed to the public and the book was a considerable success, going into a second edition in the year of publication. Bentley re-issued it in a cheap, six-shilling, form in November 1832 and the novel remained popular for many years. One of the earliest reviews (in the *Literary Gazette* on 30 January 1830) had shrewdly noted its salient virtue — Galt had 'that peculiar talent which, to this day, makes Robinson Crusoe and his lonely island a thing of tangible memory and actual existence'. The commercial scenes of *Lawrie Todd* do indeed have the sharp brilliance of Defoe.

Galt was clear of the King's Bench by early November 1829. Writing from 23 Downing Street on 28 November he told Blackwood he was 'engaged in some confidential matters' for the Board of Trade and fervently hoped for a government place — 'but few such things are going'. His flow of articles to Maga continued unabated and in such quantity that Blackwood had to send some back, and Galt, now entirely dependent on his writing, knew that he would have to look elsewhere. Maga and Blackwood had been generous, but a factory needs more than one outlet for its production.

Galt surveyed his merchandizable skills. He could write novels and he could write articles, and he had to have money. His newest novel-publishers, Colburn and Bentley, were proving lively and enterprising. To Colburn and Bentley he would go. He threw off for them another three-volume novel, *Southennan*. The writing was completed at high speed by the end of February, though publication was delayed until July. Left to his own devices, Galt had committed the foolishness of another of his historical romances, this time on the period of Mary Queen of Scots. The

Literary Gazette of 3 July, with some justification, wrote that his historical romances were 'cold, uninteresting, deficient in character and dramatic power'. It is unlikely that Galt gave the romance more than half his mind, once he had collected his advance, since he was soon deeply engaged on what for him was a much more interesting project proposed by Colburn and Bentley, a life of his old travelling companion, Lord Byron.

The contract for the life of Byron roused him from the depressed lethargy in which he had been grinding out *Southennan*. Galt was only slowly emerging from the state of shock induced by the disaster of the previous year. He had been writing, like an automaton, in lonely lodgings — 'occasionally tired of literature' — and avoiding old acquaintances. But they began to seek him out. The wealthy merchant, member of parliament and Canadian land-owner, the Right Hon. Edward Ellice, called and invited him to dinner. Others of his old acquaintances soon followed. J. G. Lockhart (co-founder in Edinburgh of Maga but resident in London since 1825 as editor of the *Quarterly Review*) was particularly concerned. He and John Murray called to offer him the editorship of the London evening newspaper, *The Courier*, at a salary of £850. Galt's family had arrived from Canada at the beginning of the summer, and the position meant security and reasonable comfort in the furnished house which Galt rented for them (at £250 a year) in Half Moon Street. Yet in July, after only two months in the position, Galt resigned.

In the *Autobiography* he gave no explanation of his decision, simply stating that 'I perceived that the business would not suit me'. There the matter would have rested had not an anonymous writer some years later published a statement that Mr Galt 'was obliged to make way'. Galt (in ill-health and now living quietly in Greenock) promptly published a full explanation in the July 1837 number of *Fraser's Magazine*: he had resigned of his own volition, on an issue of censorship, the proprietor of the newspaper, Mr William Stewart, having suppressed one of his articles after Galt had passed the proofs and gone home for the day; Galt had accepted the editorship on the explicit condition that he had 'the entire control of the paper'. He concluded his explanation by citing Horace's ode about 'the man tenacious of his purpose' *justum et tenacem propositi virum*. Galt (to use his own words)

was not 'bird-mouthed on peremptory occasions'. He might need
money, but not at the price of his integrity.

Lockhart had no patience with such scruples. He had tried to
help Galt to a secure income and — as he recounted later to
B. R. Haydon — Galt had once again thrown away the opportunity of fortune 'by quarrelling with his superiors'. At the insistence of the Secretary of the Treasury, *The Courier* as a 'government' paper had been compelled to issue falsely optimistic
bulletins on the dying George IV. To Lockhart, an astute political
journalist, this presented no problem — it was, in his opinion,
'folly' for an impecunious writer not to make 'such a sacrifice to
truth'.⁴ Galt saw it otherwise and withdrew discreetly into more
honourable writing.

He went back to work on his biography and completed it by
the end of the summer, the Preface being dated 12 August. *The
Life of Lord Byron, by John Galt, Esq.* appeared as No. 1 of a
new Colburn and Bentley low-priced (five-shillings) series, the
'National Library', in August. It created a sensation. It was
bitterly attacked and enthusiastically praised, and it kept on selling. Three editions, totalling 10,000 copies, were exhausted by the
end of 1830. It achieved a fourth edition early in 1831 and a fifth
edition in mid-year. The reason for the success is not far to seek.
Byron was news, and Galt's book was well-written, much of it
from personal knowledge. The reason for the divergent responses
is equally clear. Everyone had an extreme view on Byron. No one
was neutral. He was a hero, a villain, an aristocrat, a renegade, a
king of poets, a devil of infamy. Two of Byron's old associates —
Thomas Moore and J. C. Hobhouse — had already published a
great deal of Byron memorabilia and, almost considering they
had exclusive rights on him, openly resented Galt's intrusion.
Moore lampooned Galt in a verse in a Dublin newspaper and
Galt replied in the same spirit — and the same stanza form.
Hobhouse's criticism (partly in private letters and partly in
Colburn and Bentley's *New Monthly Magazine*) was less
friendly, and Galt first sharply replied in the same magazine
and then published the whole exchange of correspondence in
an article, 'Pot *versus* Kettle' in the December issue of *Fraser's
Magazine*.

The Life of Lord Byron is a workmanlike job. It drew openly on reminiscences of Byron that had been published since his death in 1824, and used Galt's own first-hand knowledge of him as the successful poet in London and as the traveller of the earlier cantos of *Childe Harold's Pilgrimage*. In spite of some doubts cast by his detractors, it is clear that Galt and Byron, though far apart in personality and in social position, came to know and respect each other. Galt in his biography steered clear of gossip and the scandals (real or alleged) of Byron's tempestuous life and presented a cool, independent, contemporary assessment of Byron as poet and man that still remains of basic importance. Many of the reviews of the book (and there were many) recognized Galt's achievement. The *Literary Gazette*, no automatic admirer of Galt, in a long review extending over the issues of 28 August and 4 September gave the biography 'our most cordial approbation . . . Good sense, good feeling, and good taste, go far towards making a good biographer. He possesses them all.' The September *Gentlemen's Magazine* in praising the book commented: 'Mr Galt's volume should invariably accompany the collected works of the poet, to the mischief of some of which it would act as an antidote . . . it cannot fail to be popular, for it is the only complete record extant of the whole life of one of the most remarkable men of any age or country'.

In spite of such reviews Galt — to his dismay — found the Life attacked on a bewildering variety of fronts. Some of the reviews — notably those in the *Athenaeum* of 4 September and in the October *Edinburgh Review* were really attacks on his publishers. Less enterprising firms (including John Murray, the publisher of Moore's work on Byron) were viewing with some jealousy Colburn and Bentley's success with cheap books. The *Edinburgh Review* elected to make a high moral issue of it — 'to begin a *National Library* with Lord Byron's life, argues a determination to consult only the taste and fashion of the times'. Even Christopher North, in the *Noctes Ambrosianae* of the November Maga, although paying tribute to Galt's 'extraordinary powers', found his cool man-to-man view of Byron 'ludicrous' — 'people in the humble condition of Mr Galt', the Professor of Moral Philosophy of Edinburgh University wrote solemnly, 'are not, by the rules of society, permitted to approach nobility but in a deferential attitude'. It remained for *Fraser's Magazine* to rally to Galt's defence,

which it did in a massive 24-column review in October and in a
tart article 'The Edinburgh Review *versus* Galt's Life of Byron'
in December.

Galt found it difficult to see how he could have caused such a
variety of offence. 'Why am I an object of malicious satire or
criticism?' he wrote Moir on 21 September, 'The thing is to me
somewhat inexplicable.' The truth was that *anyone* who wrote
anything on Byron at the time offended *somebody*. Everyone was
a partisan. When the fuss died down, as it had when Galt completed his *Literary Life* in 1834, he was able to see that his book
was by then 'better appreciated'. But the original hostility (quite
reasonably) annoyed him; and since, in those days before royalty
agreements, he had been paid only for his work on the first edition
he always remembered his best-seller as 'the worst paid and the
most abused' of all his books.

3

Galt was in the news, but the returns from one novel and one
biography were insufficient to support the family now reunited
(in quite expensive accommodation) in Half Moon Street. He
had to remain on the treadmill, and during the whole of 1830 —
and thereafter for several years — he ground out general articles
and short tales at a steady rate. 'I can with health', he wrote
Moir on 21 Sptember of that year, 'count on an income of at
least a thousand a year'. Blackwood at the end of 1829 had been
returning so much that Galt was forced to look for other publications that would accept the overspill. One obvious outlet was the
New Monthly Magazine, which belonged to his publishers,
Colburn and Bentley. This magazine printed, in the last three
months of 1830, his controversy with Hobhouse, a short story
'The Tales of Stamboul — Caliph Zelim' (December 1830), 'On
the Principles of Property and the Poor Law' (January 1831), a
short story 'Magrovitch, the Pole' (March 1831) with a delightful
demon who utters his demonic remarks in Gothic Black Letter,
and a 'Biographical Sketch of William Paterson, The Projector
of the Darien Company' (August 1832). *The Literary Souvenir*
(January 1830) contained a signed story 'The Confession' and
The Club-Book (July 1831) no fewer than five, 'The Unguarded

Hour', 'The Painter', 'The Book of Life', 'Haddad-ben-Ahab', and 'The Fatal Whisper'. Later he found a brief foothold in the *National Standard*, where he had two short articles (on Greek names and on the invention of printing) on 26 January and 2 February 1833. It is more than likely that other publications of this time contained anonymous material that helped him towards his target of a thousand a year.

His major source of regular income for some years was *Fraser's Magazine for Town and Country*. Fortunately for Galt, this new London magazine had started just at the moment when Blackwood was showing increasing reluctance. The proprietor, James Fraser of Regent Street, was another of the ubiquitous Scottish booksellers turned publisher, and the editor the old Maga-contributor, Dr William Maginn. Galt contributed an article to the opening number of February 1830. Thereafter, for his remaining years in London, Galt was as regular a feature of *Fraser's Magazine* as he had been earlier in *Blackwood's Magazine*. Blackwood rejected an article in March 1830 which duly made its appearance in *Fraser's Magazine* and Galt sent him no more. The correspondence between the two men ceased for over a year and two years were to elapse before there was another Galt article in Maga.

His contributions to *Fraser's Magazine* for some time drew largely on his Canadian experiences and his knowledge of colonial development. He began with easily-written 'Tales'. In February 1830 he contributed 'The Hurons — A Canadian Tale' and followed this up in April with 'Canadian Sketches No. II — The Bell of St. Regis'. Then came at intervals: 'American Traditions — Cherockee, A Tradition of the Backwoods' (October); 'Guelph in Upper Canada' (November); 'American Traditions No. II — The Early Missionaries; or the Discovery of the Falls of Niagara' (August 1831); 'American Traditions No. III — The Indian and the Hunter; or the Siege of Micford' (April 1832). He wrote a considerable group of articles on colonial policy: a series of three 'Letters on West Indian Slavery' extending over November and December 1830 and January 1831; 'Means of Lessening the West Indian Distress' (April 1831); 'The Whole West Indian Question' (July 1833); and 'The Free-Trade Question' in two articles (November 1832 and January 1833). All these articles were either signed by Galt or (by such a device as 'by the Author of *Sir Andrew Wylie*') were openly attributed to him.

There is also a set of anonymous articles in *Fraser's Magazine* of which he is demonstrably the author. 'Buckingham Palace', a London townscape article, was rejected by Blackwood on 23 March 1830 — 'it is like cutting off a portion of myself when I return any article of yours . . . I think it will answer better for a London publication'. It appeared in *Fraser's Magazine* in May; and is immediately followed by a review article 'Canadian Affairs', likely to be the 'Canada paper' which Galt offered Blackwood unsuccessfully the previous 30 December. From clues in his letters and internal evidence, one can safely also assign to him the unsigned book reviews: 'The British North American Provinces' (February 1832); 'The Canada Corn Trade' (October 1832); and 'The Greek Revolution' (February 1833). To these can be added the signed 'The Ancient Commerce of England' (November 1831), a long-preserved essay he had written about 1805 when he had been studying commercial law; an occasional letter; and a series of articles written up by the editor (e.g. that on Galt's colleague in Canada, Dr William Dunlop, in April 1833, and on Grant Thornton, the original of Lawrie Todd, in June 1833) where Galt provided the material.

It is no wonder, therefore, that the magazine rushed to the defence of his Life of Byron. He was one of the 'Fraserians', a frequenter of the dinners held in the 'back parlour' in Regent Street, his books invariably receiving long and careful reviews. In the issue of December 1830 he was given the double honour of a pen portrait (by Maginn) and an engraved line-portrait (by Maclise the staff artist) in Fraser's 'Gallery of Illustrious Literary Characters'. He was one of their mainstays.

4

While the flow of articles proceeded, Galt still accepted every contract for books that came his way. Colburn and Bentley were as insatiable as Galt was inexhaustible. When he finished the *Life of Lord Byron* in the summer of 1830, J. G. Lockhart, concerned at the failure of his *Courier* plan, suggested that Galt (ever a keen playgoer) could write a series of short biographies of actors.

Colburn and Bentley thought well of the idea, and Galt found
great pleasure in compiling 'the humours and eccentricities' for a
two-volume work, *Lives of the Players by John Galt*. It was completed by the end of the summer; delay in publication till June
1831 enabled Galt to insert a Postscript on the death of his boyhood's idol of the theatre, Mrs Siddons. The work was well
received, even by the usually hostile *Monthly Review*. The
Literary Gazette commended it as 'a capital parlour work', a
description kindly meant and precisely accurate.

Lockhart, still solicitous, proposed on 31 August 1830 a further
commission, 'a clear lively compendious account of the present
state of British Commerce and Manufactures' to be written for
Murray's 'Family Library' — Galt having had 'the Education
and habits of a merchant' could present the subject 'in a far
more intelligible as well as interesting form than any other
literateur I know of'.[5] Galt did not take up the suggestion. He was
feeling the strain. 1830 had been for him a year of indifferent
health and he had some thoughts (expressed to Moir on 21 September) of retiring quietly to Inveresk. But his boys were destined for
commercial careers and for them London was the better base;
when Colburn and Bentley came up with yet another project —
this time a sequel to the best-selling *Lawrie Todd* — Galt laid
aside his dreams of a Scottish retirement and in March 1831
moved the family from expensive Half Moon Street to Barn
Cottage in the rural area of Old Brompton. There Moir was able
to visit him and found it no more than a mile and a half's walk
from Hyde Park Corner and yet 'surrounded by nurseries and
green fields'. It was handy; it was pleasant; it was a good place
for uninterrupted writing; and it was cheap.

The sequel commissioned by Colburn and Bentley, *Bogle
Corbet or The Emigrants by John Galt*, came out in three volumes
in April 1831. It was meant to be a picture of emigrant life for a
man of Galt's own class, the Preface announcing it intended 'to
show what a person of ordinary genteel habits has really to expect
in emigrating to Canada'. There is little attempt at 'fiction' and
much of the novel is constructed from barely disguised material
he had already published in *Fraser's Magazine* and elsewhere.
The third volume, 'intended by me to be a guide book', offered
an unashamed appendix in the form of a gazetteer describing in

factual detail the different townships in Canada. The book was well reviewed; the public were interested; Galt's productivity and command of realistic detail had worn the critics down, the June *New Monthly Magazine* commenting that like Defoe Galt had 'the sheer power of *vraisemblance*'. *Bogle Corbet* did not have the run-away sales of *Lawrie Todd* but Colburn and Bentley were satisfied with their bargain.

Galt was not so satisfied. He regarded *Bogle Corbet* as 'a tolerable book'. He was also conscious that it had been produced with an 'occasional sense of drudgery'. Colburn and Bentley, he recorded in his *Literary Life*, had given orders for the three-volume novel 'like to an upholsterer for a piece of furniture'. But even in the modest retreat of Barn Cottage he was dependent on them, and in some weariness started on yet another three volumes and duly completed on 31 December 1831 (when he added the Preface) *Stanley Buxton or The Schoolfellows*, a mixture of Radcliffean ghost-machinery, changeling child, Scottish school-days, and extremely effective scenes of business and 'Grub Street' life in London. There was the usual delay while the manuscript lay on Colburn and Bentley's assembly-line and it appeared in March 1832. The reviews were again respectful. Thackeray, a fellow-Fraserian, read it immediately on publication and recorded in his diary on 5 April 'very clever though rather dull — Mr Galt knows the world or seems to know it very well'.[6] Galt would have been satisfied with this verdict. It was not the first time in his career that it took a fellow-professional to recognize his skill — even in an admittedly routine commissioned piece of writing.

By the end of 1831 Galt was heartily sick of working for Colburn and Bentley. Another year was to elapse before he could finally escape from them, with the three volumes of *Eben Erskine or The Traveller by John Galt*, largely a fictional re-hash of his Mediterranean travels, completed in the latter part of 1832 though not published till May 1833. In the Preface he announced that it 'may be my last novel'. It was certainly the last novel he undertook for Colburn and Bentley. In his later *Literary Life* Galt bluntly stated that he 'would not wish to be estimated' by these later Colburn and Bentley novels. He was under no illusions about what need had driven him to do. By late 1831 (when he had completed *Bogle Corbet*), though he had not yet quite contrived to escape from the treadmill, he was already engaged in more congenial tasks.

Galt contrived to signal his view of these commissioned pieces by the device of signing them plainly 'By John Galt' on the title page. None of his earlier novels had borne his name. They had been 'By the Author of The Ayrshire Legatees' or 'By the Author of Annals of the Parish'. Why this change of style, which began with *Lawrie Todd* and continued throughout the Colburn and Bentley series till *Eben Erskine*? It was clearly deliberate. Galt was making an announcement to the understanding reader: This work is by that public figure, John Galt, who has been publicly imprisoned for debt, and publicly discharged under the Insolvency Act. He is writing for the money he needs, to support his family and discharge his debts. It is not by the real writer who is (as all know from his title-pages) 'the Author of The Ayrshire Legatees, Annals of the Parish, Etc., Etc.'

And towards the end of 1831 the real writer quietly set to work once more.

8. *The fight back*

1831 WAS for Galt a year of mixed fortunes, some ill-health, but ultimately of rising hopes. The move to Barn Cottage had been both literally and figuratively a retreat, and for a time he saw few of his old associates in the world of affairs; the middle months of the year he later recalled as 'the most uncomfortable of my whole life'. He felt he had passed his meridian and was being 'elbowed from the thoroughfares of life'. Confidence was slowly restored. Hearing that Colburn and Bentley and Blackwood were corresponding concerning a possible reprint of his earlier novels, he wrote Oliver and Boyd (on 25 June and 4 August) about what they could do — if they did not wish to reprint, 'an Edition of the three novels might be sold' in Colburn and Bentley's *Standard Novels*. This planning for a collected edition came to nothing. Blackwood on 26 September told Galt that Colburn and Bentley's final offer 'was so unworthy of the Books that I never thought of corresponding further on the subject' — they had offered £175 for ten Blackwood titles, including five by Galt. Blackwood thought he 'could republish with advantage in cheap form' himself. Galt was cheered by the interest being shown; and further encouragement came in a lively and acute consideration of his novels in the *Noctes Ambrosianae* of the September Maga. His work and his name were not being forgotten.

What finally brought Galt back into circulation was — of all things — the Canada Company. Galt had no financial stake in its affairs and no hope of a recall to its service, but he still watched daily the price of its stock. *The Times* on 15 June announced that the court of directors had met and declared a four per cent dividend for the half year. The stock rose to par. When Galt read this, 'I saw that I might again go among my old friends, without blushing for an undertaking, the solidity of which experience had now vindicated'. He 'literally lost not an hour' in moving into action; secured from the wealthy Edward Ellice, M.P. a promise that his 350,000 acres in Canada would be available for purchase; interviewed Lord Howick at the Colonial Office and was assured that the government would offer no difficulties; persuaded a group of Members of Parliament to form a provisional committee and issue a prospectus for a proposed new land company. Galt was duly appointed secretary of what became the British American Land Company, with an office in Serle Street, Lincoln's Inn, later in Freeman's Court, Cornhill. By September he was already installed, writing his letters from the Serle Street address, and dreaming once again of vast colonial schemes.

In this mood of revived optimism, he saw his chance of an escape from the mill of Colburn and Bentley and an opportunity to write something of his own choosing, in which 'what was lost in popularity would be made up in durability'.[1] For a long time he had meditated on a political novel; power, as *The Provost* and *Sir Andrew Wylie* had shown, was a theme which held for him fascination. In late 1831, with political reform in the air in Westminster, Galt set down to write a political novel, on his own terms, unhampered either by publisher's pressure or by the three-volume tyranny, which he had complained of as early as 1824 in *Rothelan*, of the 'circulating libraries, for which all judicious authors now expressly write'. *The Member, an Autobiography* was published in one volume in January 1832. It was — the deliberate change in style on the title-page emphasized that it was the real and not the enforced writer speaking — 'By the Author of "The Ayrshire Legatees" etc. etc.' The publisher was James Fraser of Regent Street, the successful owner of *Fraser's Magazine*, a tyro in the business of novel-publishing.

The Member was immediately well received by the London journals. *The Athenaeum* (January 28) wished 'Mr Galt would do nothing but write imaginary autobiographics'. The *Literary Gazette* of the same day admired 'Mr Galt's dry humour and shrewd observation'. The March *New Monthly Magazine*, although its proprietors Colburn and Bentley had temporarily lost Galt to another publisher, warmly commended 'the peculiar manner of thought and expression which has placed Mr Galt so

high among the popular authors of the time'. The review in the
April *Fraser's Magazine* was — naturally — favourable and extended to fourteen columns, shrewdly recognizing in Galt's new
book 'the development of fresh and novel powers'. Yet in spite of
such reviews, *The Member* did not sell particularly well. Neither
did its one-volume sequel, *The Radical*, which Fraser published
in May. Fraser had the unsold sheets of both books made up into
a new single volume, re-titled *The Reform*, which he published in
November. The sales were again unsatisfactory.

This calls for some explanation. Galt's recent books had all
sold well. Why this peculiar failure, after such good reviews?
Galt was himself puzzled at the time: his friends, he noted in the
Literary Life, thought the books 'clever and philosophical'; they
attracted on the Continent 'more attention than any other products of my pen'. The failure in sales must be largely attributed
to his new publisher's lack of experience. A book needs more than
its own merits to command good sales. James Fraser was a bookseller and the proprietor of a popular magazine. But *Fraser's
Magazine*, as he advertised with some pride, was 'not connected
with any large publishing house'. This assertion — meant to
reassure readers of the magazine's independence — provides the
answer to the puzzle. Fraser was not in any major sense a book-
publisher and not in any sense a novel-publisher. The bookseller
and magazine proprietor was a novice in the field, and lacked the
sophisticated salesmanship and expertise in distribution to the
'brethren' of the trade which characterized the real professionals,
whether they were apparently restrained like Constable, Blackwood, and Cadell, or flagrant and open puffers like Colburn and
Bentley. In leaving the latter, Galt had gained his artistic freedom,
but he had to pay the price of losing their smooth efficiency. It
takes more than an author to sell a book.

These Fraser novels have never been reprinted. During the
nineteenth century, Galt was kept assiduously in print by the firm
of William Blackwood and Sons, first in their 'Standard Novels',
and later in their 1895 collected eight-volume edition of the
'Works of John Galt'. These reprints were exclusively confined to
the original Blackwood copyrights, the series that began with
The Ayrshire Legatees and concluded with *The Last of the
Lairds*. When this edition was reprinted in 1936, the old Oliver

and Boyd *Ringan Gilhaize* was added. *The Member* was forgotten
and ignored. It has been out of print for nearly a century and a
half, and few copies of its only edition are extant. As a result,
though it is one of Galt's ablest and most original books, it has
received little serious critical attention.

The Member shows Galt at his ironic best. In a self-told and
self-revealing narrative, the Scots hero Archibald Jobbry returns
moderately wealthy from India and decides to purchase a seat in
Parliament — 'my object in being at the expense of going there-
into was to make power for myself'. His canny negotiations as he
beats down the price of the sitting member, his open use of his
position for patronage — 'my object in procuring a seat was to
benefit my kith and kin'; his successful tricks in winning two
boisterous contested elections; his rise in power and influence
with Ministers; his outwitting of 'the juvenile Machiavelli that
infest the benches'; and his final prudent decision to withdraw —
just ahead of the Reform Act and the imminent dissolution of his
constituency — are done with mastery and economy. Jobbry is
not portrayed as a bad man, nor as a self-deceiver. He is as capable of kindness as of cunning. He is simply a shrewd realistic
politician of his age, who expresses his principles with Baconian
terseness — 'The young stand by principle, the old by law, the
wise by expediency, and the foolish by their own opinion'.

The sequel, *The Radical*, is less concerned with the politics of
power — indeed the hero, Nathan Butt, barely gains his seat in
Parliament when an election committee of the House ejects him,
ruling that he has been returned by perjury. Rather, it is a skilful
psychological study of the development of a natural rebel: ex-
pelled from school; self-educated on Rousseau, *Caleb Williams*
and *Political Justice*; breaking with religion; advocating 'philosophy'; delivering a speech that leads to the reading of the riot-
act; evolving into a Whig politician. Nathan Butt, the Whig
rebel, and Archibald Jobbry, the Tory dispenser of 'places', are
considerable creations, every bit as well done as the Rev. Micah
Balwhidder and Mr Pawkie. Their disappearance from the roll of
memorable nineteenth-century novel characters is due to a simple
accident in publishing.

Galt in these novels — but more particularly in *The Member*
— shows remarkable originality. *The Member* is the first political

novel in English. *Coningsby* did not appear till 1844. Mr Jobbry's two election contests in the rotten borough of Frailtown are as lively as anything in the Eatanswill election in *Pickwick Papers*, written five years later. In *The Member* Galt has effortlessly expanded the frontiers of the English novel, which from Richardson onwards had been a domestic story, with love and marriage as the necessary centre. Galt's two political novels are on professional life, not domestic; men at work, not men in love. It was an area of human experience that would not be fully exploited till Conrad began writing at the end of the century.

2

With the rise in his public fortunes and an office in town, Galt was able to re-emerge into the social life of London. Carlyle recorded in his notebook for 21 January 1832 that he met him (with Hogg and Lockhart) at a Fraser's dinner with 'the air of a sedate Greenock Burgher; mouth indicating sly humour and self-satisfaction . . . peaceable, clear, gutmüthig'.[2] A few nights later the revived Galt attended an equally *gutmüthig* but less sedate function. The *Literary Gazette* of 28 January reported the 'Scottish Literary Dinner' of the 25th: Galt's health was pledged 'near the witching hour' and (in the customary drunken confusion of Burns Night) 'Galt's thanks died in embryo'. At a more sober function on 17 May, Henry Crabb Robinson met him and — his note reveals much of both writers — found Galt 'in his manner quiet and well-behaved; neither rude nor servile though a Scotchman'.[3] Galt was back in town, poised and assured in his official position, moving freely among old friends and new acquaintances.

The poor sales of *The Member* and *The Radical* meant he still had to supplement his income, and he was forced to accept another commission. The partnership of Colburn and Bentley having dissolved at the end of August 1832 when Bentley bought out his partner,[4] Galt threw off for the new owner during the year, with little interest in the task, the three volumes of *Eben Erskine*, his final commissioned novel 'By John Galt'. Bentley then drew up a memorandum of agreement (dated 6 October 1832) for the purchase of the copyright of *Lawrie Todd*, for the sum of £25. Galt — as the original agreement (now in the National Library of Scotland)[5] shows — refused to part with the copyright and allowed instead an edition of 10,000 copies. It was published in November as No. 21 of 'Bentley's Standard Novels'. Galt continued his regular articles for *Fraser's Magazine*, and with the help of a friend, Andrew Picken, he gathered together a collection of Canadian material which appeared in June under Picken's editorship as *The Canadas . . . from original documents furnished by John Galt*. All of this was merely what had to be done, and none of it was written with any sense of commitment.

What Galt really wanted to do was to write another work of his own choice, which would develop — in the context of the politics of 1832 — the Scottish small town life of his early successes with Blackwood. One of his sons had been in Scotland during the summer and was kindly received by the Blackwood family. This led to a resumption of correspondence, and Blackwood on 24 July suggested that Galt might be induced 'to take up the pen for Maga once more'. Nothing could have fitted in better with Galt's own wishes and he replied promptly on 31 July suggesting a new series 'Our Borough'. The first portion was speedily dispatched and Blackwood on 24 August proclaimed with his old enthusiasm 'This is your own undisputed field'. He waited till Galt sent him more portions, and chapters I–III of 'Our Borough By the Dean of Guild' appeared in the October number.

It was without indication of authorship, and indeed none was necessary. In these admirable opening chapters of vintage Galt, the Tory Town Council of a small Ayrshire borough decides that since the Whigs are in power it would be discreet to change allegiance, and Robin Gables, the politic Dean of Guild, is deputed to go to London to treat with Earl Grey. Mrs Gables is to be left behind — but she has her own ideas. 'One of your chef d'ouevres', wrote Blackwood with delight. He had re-captured the genuine Galt.

What Blackwood did not know was that he was not the only one. Yet another Edinburgh bookseller with publishing ambitions had entered the field. William Tait, of 78 Princes Street, issued in April 1832 the first number of a new journal, *Tait's Edinburgh Magazine*. Although its politics were Whig, *Tait's Edinburgh Magazine* secured Galt as a contributor in its very first volume.

Tait wrote Galt requesting an article, and the reply of 12 July was enthusiastic — 'I shall be very happy to send you now and then an article in that peculiar style which you wish'. He offered Tait 'The Howdie'. 'Of course', added the Tory author to his new Whig publisher, 'it has nothing political in it.'[6] Tait made an offer of ten guineas — 'but whatever Fraser pays you I will pay' — and 'The Howdie An Autobiography' appeared anonymously in the September and October issues. Galt nowhere in his lists of works lays claim to 'The Howdie', but the correspondence between the two men establishes its authenticity, confirmed when a section of the original manuscript in Galt's hand found its way to Sotheby's in 1920. This fragment was in 1923 edited by W. Roughead as an 'unpublished' Galt manuscript. The full text, in *Tait's Edinburgh Magazine*, has never been reprinted.

It must be asked, since Blackwood was begging Galt to take up the pen for Maga once more, why he was not sent 'The Howdie'? Galt was only too well aware of the chaste conventions imposed on Maga contributors. Blackwood and his editorial helpers in the back room of 45 George Street knew that Galt could over-step their code and be (in Blackwood's guarded words) 'perhaps a little strong'. Christopher North, the mouthpiece of the group, expressed the ambivalent but official Maga view of Galt in the *Noctes Ambrosianae* of November 1830. There (in his own person) he proclaimed 'Mr Galt is a man of genius'. To this he put an immediate rejoinder in the mouth of the Ettrick Shepherd, James Hogg — 'He's aften unco coorse'. Galt had not forgotten Blackwood's horror at the first draft of *The Last of the Lairds*, from which Dr Moir had felt impelled to prune what he called its 'vulgarity and uncleanness'. How then could Galt send Blackwood his latest work, the richly comic autobiography of a midwife (a 'howdie') relating her experiences with the frank and earthy gusto of the Wife of Bath? The surprising thing is that in 1832 it was printed in any middle-class monthly magazine.

Rural Ayrshire — as Burns had earlier discovered — was not polite Edinburgh. Mrs Blithe, the howdie, practises her profession in rural Ayrshire. Blackwood could never have printed her lively chronicle of the lying-in of Mrs Facings, who was 'no better than a light woman'; of her Captain, who 'was not her gudeman'; of the death in childbed of Mally Stoups; of the unperturbed Lizzy

Dadily and her grandmother's 'souple trick' to secure the delivery
'free gratis for no fee at all' of her 'bastard brat'; of a baby born
in wedlock — and in church — the resourceful minister bidding
the congregation 'skail' — 'on account of the visible working of
Providence in the midst of us'; of the young Miss who ailed and
disappeared to Glasgow to return 'as slimb as a poplar tree' and
in due course adopted her distant cousin's 'wee fatherless and
motherless orphan'. Mrs Blithe's comic repertoire is inexhaustible.
'The Howdie', with its blend of humour and compassion, of
simple acceptance of a real situation, is — for any writer, and
especially for a male author — an astonishing piece of virtuosity
and skilful writing. It is the annals of a parish that the Rev.
Micah Balwhidder knew, but preferred not to recount, and
Blackwood certainly never would have accepted.

Galt had two supporters in Edinburgh who had less genteel
views than the Maga group. William Tait was a rival of Blackwood, both in business and in the politics of the Town Council.
Something of a rebel himself (he spent four days in jail in 1833
for refusing to pay church rates) he was happy to welcome a
lively piece of uninhibited writing — particularly by a noted
Maga contributor. Galt's other supporter was the middle-aged,
twice-married, Mrs Christian Isobel Johnstone, a lady from Fife.
After her second marriage to the schoolmaster John Johnstone,
the pair purchased a newspaper, the *Inverness Courier*, and the
Dictionary of National Biography records that she gave the paper
'a more literary turn than was customarily attained by a provincial newspaper'. It was for this journal that she wrote in the
issue of 10 May 1821 — on her own initiative and far from the
literary Capital — the first enthusiastic and percipient review of
Annals of the Parish, which had so gratified Blackwood. Thereafter she remained a sensitive and ultimately outspoken devotee
of Galt.

When the Johnstones moved to Edinburgh to acquire a printing
office, they became — their radical political views being congenial — the printers of *Tait's Edinburgh Magazine*. Mrs
Johnstone in the same year 1832 established her own magazine,
The Schoolmaster and Edinburgh Weekly Magazine which after
a short time was converted into a monthly, *Johnstone's Edinburgh
Magazine*. In 1834 her magazine was absorbed into *Tait's*

Edinburgh Magazine. In the language of today it was a reverse
take-over. Mrs Johnstone became half owner and sole editor, and
remained in charge till the magazine was sold in 1846. This
formidable lady, editor, author, promoter of cheap books, novelist,
and proprietor in her own right (nonetheless, as De Quincey,
who wrote for her, noted, 'with absolutely no sacrifice or loss of
feminine dignity') published Galt's best work in his later years.
His 'vulgarity' she found admirable. During 1832 she was working closely with William Tait, and although she did not assume
the full editorship till some time later, it is likely that she was
behind Tait's initial approach to Galt.

3

With such support from both of Edinburgh's major magazines,
Galt was poised for a return to real writing. At this moment fate
dealt him a vicious blow. At the beginning of October 1832 he
suffered a stroke — one of a series — and was for a time helpless
with paralysis. Galt had been ill at various times in his life. Like
many active and restless people, he suffered from a vague malaise
('all-overishness' he called it) when things went against him;
activity and fresh interest soon restored him. There was nothing
psychosomatic about arteriosclerosis, which at first crippled him
completely. He gradually regained the use of his legs — and
doggedly walked to his town office — but for over a year he could
not effectively use his pen. He managed, with difficulty, to append
his initials to the Bentley agreement of 6 October. His extant
letters from October 1832 till late in 1833 are generally in another
hand, sometimes with a shaky signature at the end. His literary
work — which continued voluminous — was almost entirely dictated.

The literary output of this year of illness was, not unnaturally,
of no great quality. Galt wrote — dictated rather — compulsively,
driven by his innate energy and the needs of his family. He made
considerable use of the mass of papers he had accumulated and
refurbished much old material. At first he tried to continue with
his work for both Edinburgh magazines. But Blackwood on
24 November was 'disappointed in these last Chapters' and
printed no more of 'The Borough'; Tait was similarly forced to

send back the proffered third part of 'The Howdie'.⁷ Galt, un-
deterred, turned to his pile of papers and re-shaped his old
dramatic venture of 1828, 'An Aunt in Virginia', into an amusing prose-sketch 'Scotch and Yankees'. Blackwood cheerfully
acepted and paid for it on 22 December. Galt followed this up
with a second 'national' caricature, a comic highlander the
central figure, entitled 'The Chief'. Blackwood again accepted
this 'odd and amusing extravaganza'. 'Scotch and Yankees A
Caricature' (by 'the Author of Annals of the Parish') appeared in
the January and February 1833 numbers of Maga. 'The Chief;
or, The Gael and the Sassenach, in the Reign of George IV
A Caricature' appeared without indication of authorship in the
numbers of April and May.

Galt might be physically handicapped and unable to use his
pen, but he planned and produced in quantity with his old
tenacity. The publishing firm of Smith Elder had offices in Cornhill near those of the British America Land Company and this
may have led him to agree to write a one-volume story for their
series, 'The Library of Romance'. He dictated a sedately-told
romantic tale, *The Stolen Child*, on the theme of a long-lost heir,
the romantic hero off-set by a downright Scottish housekeeper,
Mrs Servit. Galt added the preface on 26 March 1833 and the
book appeared that month. For a work of no special merit, *The
Stolen Child* was generously received, notably in the June *Tait's
Edinburgh Magazine*, where the comment that the 'Scottish
housekeeper shows the pencil of the Author of Annals of the
Parish' indicates the hand of Mrs Johnstone. The generous notice
must have prompted him to send something to the magazine. He
had nothing new to offer, but *Tait's Edinburgh Magazine* published in August an unsigned fantasy story 'The Extinguishers',
which Galt had mentioned he had completed in a letter to Blackwood as far back as 14 December 1820. *Tait's Edinburgh
Magazine* in September then went out of its way in an article,
'Fashionable Novelism', to introduce a reference to *The Stolen
Child*. Galt's new supporters were working on his behalf.

On 7 March Galt began a series of letters to Blackwood concerning 'a joint venture projected by me and Mr Martin'. Galt
was aiming high. The painter and engraver, John Martin, was in
1833 at the height of his fame and could command considerable

fees. Blackwood, however (18 March), had 'a horror in meddling with Engraving expenses' — the 'gentlemen of the burin' were 'vexatious and unprofitable' — he would publish on behalf of the author and artist but refused any financial responsibility in the undertaking. In May he duly published *The Ouranoulogos or The Celestial Volume*, a massive book of Martin engravings illustrating a story by Galt, 'The Deluge'. Blackwood's commercial instinct was, as usual, right. The book was a disastrous failure.

Galt's next offer to Blackwood (on 27 April) was a 'German tale of the Reformation'. He described it as a 'work that I have lately finished' — an ambiguous description of an old manuscript revamped. On this offer, Blackwood preserved a discreet silence. The economical Galt saw another use for the old tale. His two eldest sons, John (aged 19) and Thomas (aged 18) wanted to return to Canada and establish themselves in a country they remembered with pleasure. They were both to secure positions with the Canada Company. In the *Literary Life* Galt recounts that 'the outfit of my two sons occasioned an extra expense', and to meet this he contracted with yet another set of London-Scottish publishers, Cochrane and McCrone, to produce a collection of stories in three volumes. Since the sons had already sailed when Galt wrote Moir on 25 April and the work was not published till November, he must have secured an immediate advance — and then turned to his old papers for material.

The resultant *Stories of the Study* opens with a frank preface in which Galt complains of the need of the trade for 'the fashionable quantity' of three volumes. Then follows an Introduction in which he explains that, confined to his study and looking over old papers, he found 'a number of works long cast aside and forgotten'. Over half the space in the three volumes is given to 'The Lutherans' — the German tale unsuccessfully offered to Blackwood. The remainder — with a few outstanding exceptions — is an undistinguished gathering in the various genres that he had been turning out in the past few years for *Fraser's Magazine* — oriental fables, Canadian tales and the rest. For good measure he even included a story by his youngest son and the text of the ill-fated and 'still-born' 'The Deluge'.

Fortunately, he enlivened this dull mixture with three excellent stories (a combination of old material and recent writing) in Scots. 'The Seamstress', an off-shoot from *Annals of the Parish*, has an interesting introduction in which Galt notes 'the fortunate circumstance of the Scotch possessing the whole range of the English language, as well as their own'. 'The Jaunt' is a re-working of Galt's Mediterranean voyages, completely revivified by being put in the mouth of Bailie Daidles of Inverskip. 'The Dean of Guild or Mr Wamle's Journey' is essentially the material he had sent to Maga in continuation of 'the Borough'. Blackwood made one of his few errors of judgment in refusing this lively trip of a Glasgow politician to the metropolis. The ironic handling of the wily Scots politician's reaction to Reform was probably too much for the Tory Town Councillor, William Blackwood. The Whig Town Councillor, William Tait, would have leapt at the opportunity to print it.

This small group of three good stories embedded in hundreds of pages of undistinguished work was welcomed with notices of unusual warmth and generosity. The *Literary Gazette* gave it two articles, on 30 November and 7 December. The *New Monthly Magazine* for January 1834 hastened to 'congratulate Mr Galt on his re-appearance'. The reason for the welcome is made clear in the notice in *Tait's Edinburgh Magazine* for January 1834 — 'We rejoice to see Mr Galt so far recovered as to fairly outrun the critics'. There had been universal sympathy with Galt during his long illness of 1833 and admiration for his courage. Though every review properly singled out 'The Jaunt' and 'The Dean of Guild', the notices were not really a tribute to *Stories of the Study*. They were a tribute to Galt the man and his refusal to accept defeat.

The *Monthly Magazine* reviewed the collection at particular length in January 1834. It is true that this magazine had been taken over that month by Cochrane and McCrone and there was thus a further reason for printing a good review. But the unsigned article is no mercenary puff. It is a critical essay, entitled 'Genius of Galt', assessing his whole life-work, generous, acutely aware of where Galt's real strength lay and yet accepting that 'any man who has written so copiously as the author of "The Annals of the Parish" must of necessity have written unequally. The human mind cannot sustain such unremitting efforts, as he has made for so lengthened a period, without suffering exhaustion'. The reviewer then deals briefly and sensitively with Galt's salient skills, his command of narrative, his ability to create character so that 'Mr Galt himself is utterly lost sight of', and his handling of language 'with a truth and faithfulness which cannot be surpassed', before turning to praise his labour and his fortitude. It is the best assessment of Galt's work that had appeared, since Jeffrey's article in the *Edinburgh Review* in 1823.

Fraser's Magazine remained loyal during Galt's year of illness. Between January and July it printed four of his general articles, including one, 'The Whole West Indian Question', which had been offered to Blackwood and refused. As Galt was working through his old material he came across three further stories, all of which made an appearance in *Fraser's Magazine* in the latter part of the year. 'The Joke' in September was a variation on his old theme of Scots landlady and young man in London. 'My Father's House' in October was a dullish 'tale'. The third is preceded by the account of a visit to Barn Cottage paid by 'Oliver Yorke' (the 'editor' of *Fraser's Magazine*) to acquire for a hundred guineas a 'trunk-full' of Galt's 'old scraps'. This account — no doubt by Maginn — contains a great deal of playful exaggeration (which may even extend to the hundred guineas). But the December story, 'The Gudewife', is an admirable short 'autobiography' of a wife's wiles to gain the upper hand on her husband and a return to the Ayrshire scene of the old Galt that amply justifies its simple announcement of authorship — 'By the Author of Annals of the Parish'.

Galt had not yet exhausted the possibilities of his trunk-full of old papers. The manuscript life of Grant Thorburn, which he had purchased in America and then used as a source for *Lawrie Todd*, was published in December by Fraser with an introduction by Galt in a volume entitled *Forty Years in America*. Galt also made a 'collection of some poetical scraps which I found lying about' and — Blackwood not being tempted by the offer — Cochrane and McCrone published these in October as *Poems by John Galt*. They are no more than the work of a very modest versifier in Scots and English. The only permanent significance of the volume is the valuable check-list of his entire published works in the final pages. The reviewers were decently silent;

or alternatively they took the line of the *Literary Gazette* on 26 October — 'judgment is mixed with many human and kindly feelings'. Everyone knew that Galt was selling off his literary bits and pieces. No one had the heart to say more.

4

Early in 1833 as he searched through his hoarded papers, Galt came to see that they contained more than old but saleable fiction. There were documents concerned with his early travels and his dealings with the Canada Company and letters he had received from many of his friends and acquaintances. All these, and the enforced periods of immobility, led him to begin dictating his autobiography. The 'amanuensis was a boy' — Alexander, the bright fifteen-year-old youngest son. Galt dictated at intervals throughout the first half of 1833 and the work was almost entirely in print by August. Some early copies were released late that month by the publishers, Cochrane and McCrone, for review purposes. The full publication of *The Autobiography of John Galt* in two volumes took place in September, the preface being dated 12 September 1833. The work was dedicated to Ellice.

The contemporary reception was encouraging — 'it was decidedly received with kindness . . . I feel myself under many obligations to the public press', Galt wrote a year later in his *Literary Life*. The only sour note was struck in October in the always hostile *Monthly Review*, which harshly concluded that Galt was 'now roused from his dream, and by the description of his fortunes leaves a beacon of everlasting warning to youth'. This uncalled-for unpleasantness was not the typical reaction. In Scotland, as might be expected, Mrs Johnstone rallied to his support in the October *Johnstone's Edinburgh Magazine* with a long review which stated roundly 'there is no living writer whose works have afforded so much pleasure to the mass of his countrymen'. Her hand can also be detected in the equally enthusiastic review in the November *Tait's Edinburgh Magazine*, where the only complaint is that 'the hero of the piece . . . is kept too much in the background', a clear echo of her comment in October — 'it is autobiography before the curtain'. Maga, somewhat surprisingly — but William Blackwood was ill — took no notice. In

London, the *New Monthly Magazine* in October praised the
book as an 'honest autobiography' and the *Literary Gazette*
spread an enthusiastic notice of this book by 'our estimable
friend' over the three issues of 31 August, 14 September and
21 September. *Fraser's Magazine* was loyal — but inhibited by
its self-denying ordinance against puffing its own contributors.
Maginn in the December issue managed to get round this with
his usual adroitness by recounting how 'Oliver Yorke' had been
compelled to offer resistance to James Fraser's suggestion that
'our independent principles' might be for once suspended and a
'favourable review' written — 'especially as all the press has
been very kind and cordial'. In this skilful and waggish manner
he contrived to get in a good notice for Galt under the guise of a
stout refusal to depart from 'the strictness of our integrity'. The
net result was that a second edition was called for in November,
and Galt was able to tell Blackwood on 18 January of the following year 'the sale of the autobiography is satisfactory'. It was a
fitting conclusion to a year of unremitting work done in the most
difficult and often painful circumstances.

Later readers of Galt have not found the *Autobiography* of the
same interest and it has never been reprinted. It is, however, an
important — though one-sided — piece of documentation. On
his private life, he preserves absolute reticence. 'This Autobiography does not consist of confessions, but only of such a
series of transactions as may be candidly related.' The emphasis is
on Galt as he preferred to see himself, the public figure and man
of affairs. His writings receive the minimum of attention, many
are omitted entirely, and the important two chapters, 'Reflections
on my own works', occupy only 16 pages out of the 800 of the
two volumes. Galt was intent on explaining and justifying his
public career (to which his literary activity was in this context
merely incidental) and more than half of the work is concerned
with his part in Canadian affairs, documented with great
thoroughness. One can see why later readers of *Annals of the
Parish* were disappointed in Galt's apparent lack of interest in
what alone has preserved his reputation.

Yet, for the full understanding of Galt's writing, the *Autobiography* is important, and it has been used and cited extensively
in the present study. So long as the circumstances in which it was

written are kept in mind, it is a valuable, often irreplaceable, document. It does require caution in use and interpretation. Galt composed it by dictation, sometimes when ill in bed; he sent off each portion for final printing as soon as Alexander had made a fair copy; he was quite unable to maintain his usual careful proof-correction; he was often helpless with pain, and towards the end his eyes failed completely. The book was, as a consequence, never revised as a whole, and there are both duplications and omissions. From time to time (as his actual letters at the time of specific events show) he was imprecise about dates and even the sequence of events. It was, he fully expected, his last book, and his memory had become, understandably, selective as he wrote what was to be the *apologia pro vita sua*. But a study of Galt's literary career would be impossible without it.

Galt had fought back successfully. He had escaped from Colburn and Bentley and had found time to write as he wanted. Even the catastrophe of a year of illness had not diminished his output. He had paid his way, educated his three sons, and outfitted two of them for a successful career; before the year was over he had worked off all his secured debts. And, dramatically, in December 1833, his health suddenly improved. 'My improvement', he wrote Blackwood on 18 January 1834, 'has been almost as striking as the strokes'. Young Alexander, keen to follow his brothers to Canada, was offered a position in the British America Land Company, and Galt wrote Blackwood on 30 January full of bustling new plans: he was well advanced with a new book and 'I am going to Canada where two of my sons already are and the youngest is nominated to a place in the service of the new Company there'. Against all the odds, Galt was back in business.

9. *Autumn*

AS HE recovered at the end of 1833, Galt bounced back into activity. Many of his friends had regretted the limited scope of the *Autobiography*. Galt rapidly wrote a second autobiography and on 18 January 1834 offered it to Blackwood — 'I have been induced by many representations to draw up my Literary History which has grown into as much as an 8vo volume . . . it will make a work complete within itself . . . what will you give me for it?' It was published as his *Literary Life* in August, his final work under the Blackwood imprint.

With the steady rise in Galt's literary reputation, the publication of the *Literary Life* should have completed its consolidation, particularly after the satisfactory reception and sales of two printings of the *Autobiography*. Galt wrote his new book with care. He meant it for serious attention, and signalled his view of its importance by securing permission for a royal dedication. His major novel, *The Entail*, had been dedicated to George IV. The *Literary Life*, the major statement of his literary credo, was dedicated to William IV. But the preparation and printing of the book was to be attended by a series of delays, miscalculations, errors of judgment, and disasters that resulted in the ultimate issuing of the book becoming one of those publishing catastrophes to which Galt seemed prone.

Galt himself was responsible for the major error. He had offered the *Literary Life* to Blackwood on 18 January to be published 'in a volume or in the magazine'. A few days later, his son Alexander was promised a place with the British American Land Company and Galt decided to go with him in the summer to Canada. Hastily — and disastrously — changing his entire publication plans, he withdrew on 30 January the offer to Blackwood and resolved to issue 'by subscription on my own account'. Although experience should have warned him, he fell once again into the three-volume trap, and planned an extended work, *Literary Life and Miscellanies*, made up of the new autobiography bulked out with a couple of volumes of further gatherings from his apparently inexhaustible store. Blackwood agreed to publish the three volumes on joint account, offered an advance of £250 to be set off against future profits,[1] and drew up a full page advertisement for the April number of Maga. Galt received £150 to account on 22 March. By then he had 'a Law stationer copying MSS' from his hoard. His friends were circularized, and at the end of March there were enough subscriptions to pay the cost of publication. A broadsheet prospectus, with a list of subscribers, was printed off to attract public sales.

Galt's plans were again disrupted. The Company sent Alexander to Canada 'on the shortest possible notice' in early March. Galt, as he wrote Moir, 'a little flattish since parting from Alexander', gave up Barn Cottage, moved to central London, and (Blackwood urging him on strongly) prepared to leave for Scotland to supervise the printing of the three volumes. Even then some of his government friends with interests in Ireland made a bid to retain him in London on further public business 'to superintend the getting up of a Company'. Galt knew that a third secretaryship was beyond him. He was in better health, but for how long? 'It comes too late', he wrote sadly to Moir.

Galt had finally decided the time had come to quit the London scene. His sons were all placed and no longer needed his support. He could see his way to living modestly but comfortably in retirement. His wife's annuity from Dr Tilloch's estate was irregularly paid, but could generally be depended on. He could write. He had, on his mother's death (when he was in better circumstances) yielded to his sister his half-share in Captain Galt's estate and in the family house in Greenock. The house was large enough for all. His decision to move was confirmed when he heard that the Government had 'come to a resolution to make a provision for me', with a payment of £200 in April. The newspapers announced that he had been granted a government annuity. Galt could retire with honour.

The pressure proved too much. His wife Elizabeth wrote

Blackwood on 10 April[2] that Galt had 'another slight shock' and
he lay helpless in lodgings in the Strand till early June. He
struggled on with his old manuscripts and sent batches of them to
Edinburgh at frequent intervals, his friend Ellice (now Secretary
at War) providing franking facilities for the bulky packages.
Blackwood on 18 April was ready to go ahead at speed —
'Ballantyne', he promised, 'will put a great many compositors on
the work'. Then silence fell. Galt, in despair, dictated a series of
letters in April and May — he is 'wearying for proofs' — his
subscribers are in 'much perplexity' — the delay 'does me much
harm with some of my friends'. He lay in bed, fretting.

Blackwood, too, had been stricken. He, too, was helpless and in
pain, in what was to be his final illness. He recovered enough to
dictate a letter to Galt on 24 May — he rejoiced that Government
at last has 'done you some justice' — 'there is much in the Life
that is delightful' — but he is disappointed with some of the
collected material and has given the manuscript to Moir to see if
he can revise it — where is the list of subscribers? — 'I hope and
trust you will soon be able to set out for Scotland'. Galt, in London, unable to endure the agony of a coach journey, was helped
aboard the Leith steam packet by his wife and his old servant Ben
and early in June was in lodgings in Hill Street, Edinburgh, a
hundred yards distant from Blackwood's house at 3 Ainslie Place.

The two old men — old adversaries and old friends — never
saw each other again. Each was too ill to move. 'Day after day,'
Dr Moir recorded, 'my professional duties as well as my friendship led me to visit each; and it afforded me a melancholy pleasure
to carry from one invalid to the other the courtesies of mutual
regard, and the kindest wishes for restored health'.[3] Galt, assisted
by Moir, completed his three volumes, corrected his proofs, and
with his wife and Ben left for Greenock in early August. There
was no restored health for Blackwood. He died on 16 September.
It was a sad end to a good partnership.

In contrast to the success of the *Autobiography*, the *Literary
Life and Miscellanies* when published in August was — as
Blackwood had foreseen — a commercial failure. The two extra
volumes of old material were made up of pitiful savings, verse-
dramas, old commercial essays, poems, a 'History of Sugar', even
the ancient history of the Seven Years War which Galt had

written in the boredom of Gibraltar in 1812; they were lightened only by one magnificent Scots story, 'The Betheral', which the dying Blackwood (a good publisher to the end) commended as 'in your own genuine style'. Otherwise, the *Miscellanies* were precisely what the title implied.

In the final confused dealings between two sick old men, the sheet of subscribers' names went astray, and the work appeared without the customary list. It is now possible to retrieve the names of Galt's supporters, since a copy of the printed prospectus has survived among the Blackwood papers.[4] The hundred subscribers[5] listed on this broadsheet represent the world of Galt's lifelong aspirations, solid people of affairs — lawyers, men of business, gentlemen, Members of Parliament, twenty titled members of the nobility. From the literary world there is only one name, the faithful J. G. Lockhart.

Whatever caused the confusion, the loss of the list proved the final disaster. William IV got his copy, and so too — after some urging by Galt — did his sons in Canada. But many of Galt's friends had not received their copies a year after publication. 'Those hobgoblins the young Blackwoods have totally neglected the subscribers', Galt wrote Lockhart on 28 March 1836.[6] It is not possible to apportion blame with any certainty. The venture had been dogged by ill-luck from the outset. The two Blackwood sons did not share their father's faith in Galt and Galt's own decision to add two volumes of sheer ballast was enough in itself to sink the *Literary Life*.

As was common with subscription publications, few — if any — review copies were sent out. Two London journals did give the book a review: the *Literary Gazette* on 6 September applauded 'our old friend'; the *Monthly Review* (hitherto hostile to Galt) in November was unexpectedly fulsome — 'He who wrote the Annals of the Parish has long been the object of our kindliest feelings and elevated respect'. Otherwise there was silence. It was another publishing disaster.

In the end Galt came round to see that he had a responsibility for the failure and as late as 12 August 1836 he wrote the 'young Blackwoods' suggesting that the *Literary Life* be issued as a separate volume. One can hardly blame the hobgoblins for turning a deaf ear. The firm had lost money on the venture and continued for some years to bill Galt for what was still outstanding of his advance of £250. The Blackwood sons, now the proprietors of *Blackwoods' Magazine*, had their own new authors — Michael Scott, Joanna Baillie, Mrs Hemans. They had no interest in the 'Author of Annals of the Parish'. In their opinion Galt's day was done.

2

In spite of this publishing disaster, the first volume, the *Literary Life*, is a well-written book and an important piece of documentation for nineteenth-century literary studies. The elegiac overtones of the *Autobiography* have disappeared, and the new volume has a sparkle and crispness lacking in the wearily dictated volumes of the earlier life. Galt was in good fettle during the winter months of 1833-4 when he wrote the *Literary Life*. His earlier lapses of memory have disappeared, and a biographer finds no necessity to correct from other sources. In writing his 'literary life' Galt did not attempt to document his entire output as a writer. He makes no pretence of cataloguing his massive magazine contributions, content simply to note from time to time that he 'wrote for the periodicals'. The *Literary Life* is concerned with John Galt, writer of books. Like the *Autobiography*, it is an *apologia*, though it offers a different hero. The business-man who writes as a sideline is replaced by the hard-working professional writer. Galt's concern in both books is to present himself in a favourable light. In the *Literary Life* he does so, firmly, modestly, and with remarkable self-detachment.

Galt's letters and the extant manuscripts that he sent to publishers demonstrate clearly that he had (like Scott) an unusual facility in covering page after page with rapidly written narrative and dialogue, ready — without need of revision — for the printer. The quality of what was so written depended on Galt's involvement with his theme. He wrote with a running pen the great passages of *The Entail*; the manuscript of *Ringan Gilhaize*[7] has pages of excellent dialogue without one single correction; with the same facility — but without involvement — he dashed off the facile banalities of *Eben Erskine*. Galt in the *Literary Life* makes it clear that he is never taken in by this easy flow. He is a shrewd

critic of his own performance, well aware of the difference between producing so many pages of penmanship at £10 per sheet
or three-volume Colburn and Bentley novels at £300 apiece and
writing (the phrase is his own) 'con amore' on a theme and in a
format of his own choosing.

He offers in the *Literary Life* a description of each of his books
and of the circumstances that led to its composition, concluding
with an assured judgment on its merits. His assessments of his own
achievement are more accurate than those of his contemporaries.
He knew — as the journals of the time did not — when he was
merely writing competent hack-work, on which he 'would not
wish to be estimated'. On the books that mattered, he is in no
doubt. Where his judgment on these coincides with that of his
contemporaries — as with *The Entail* and *Annals of the Parish* —
his assessment is quite independent. Where he differs — as he
does with *The Member* and *Ringan Gilhaize*; or where he firmly
gives pride of place to *The Provost* over *Annals of the Parish* —
Galt's views command respect and attention.

He had come to see that he had created a new genre of fiction.
In his general assessment of his Ayrshire novels (written on the
basis of the earlier 'Reflections on my own work' in the *Autobiography*) he modestly suggests they are not novels at all: 'The
Annals of the Parish and the Provost have been generally received as novels, and I think, in consequence, they have both
suffered, for neither of them have, unquestionably, a plot. My
own notion was to exhibit a kind of local theoretical history, by
examples, the truth of which would at once be acknowledged.
But as novels they are regarded, and I must myself as such now
consider them; but still something is due to the author's intention,
for, notwithstanding the alleged liveliness of some of the sketches,
as stories they are greatly deficient.' In spite of the diffidence of
this language, Galt knew — and Coleridge knew — that he had
expanded the frontiers of the English novel.

10. *Indian Summer*

1

ALL BIOGRAPHERS of Galt have written him off at this point. Moir, who produced the earliest life, named no works after 1834 and devoted in a *Memoir* of over a hundred pages only a few paragraphs to the years between 1834 and 1839 — 'any change in his health', he wrote of these final years, 'was to the worse, not to the better'. R. K. Gordon's life of 1920 accepted this view and covered the same period in a few sentences. The standard picture of Galt in retirement in Greenock is of a failing old man, unable to hold a pen, steadily going downhill, his work in the past. W. Roughead, who owned the manuscript of 'A Rich Man' (written in what he describes as 'Galt's beautiful running script') was consequently led to assert in his edition of the story that in spite of its date of printing in 1836 its composition must be 'before he was disabled by the paralysis that compelled him to dictate all his later work'. J. W. Aberdein's biography of 1836 simply and bluntly states 'To literature Galt contributed nothing considerable after 1834. How could he?'

The facts are altogether different. After the departure for Greenock, Moir did not meet Galt again. He fell out of touch with Galt's activity in retirement, and the *Memoir*, ill-informed at this point, has led later biographers astray. In the light of fresh manuscript and printed evidence, the picture of the later Galt must now be drastically revised. Galt retired to Greenock, where he and his wife organized the old family home into two households with separate entrances. He promptly moved for a couple of months to the resort of Gourock. He was able to allow his old servant Ben to return to England, bearing a letter (dated 3 September) to a friend, John Reynolds: Galt recommended Ben for employment, 'though a groom a good personal servant', and reported on his own progress — 'though still lame I am much better than when I left London'.[1] On 27 November he wrote the 'young Blackwoods' that he was 'so much better being enabled to take exercise by machinery'. On 31 December he offered them the 'first of a series of papers for the magazine'. Galt was never to be free from the effects of arteriosclerosis and sometimes had to take to his bed. He was never idle, continued to write, and continued for several more years to be published.

Galt provides his own evidence of all this. During those occasions when he had to retreat to bed in the next few months, he found verse easier than prose and employed his time composing a series of poems in English and Scots. He had them printed in a little volume, *Efforts By an Invalid*, in Greenock in March 1835; James Fraser took over a set of sheets and issued in May a London edition with a variant title-page. The verses are of no great consequence — the *Literary Gazette* of 2 May simply offered 'kind wishes'. What is important is Galt's preface. He explains that he finds composing verses an agreeable activity when he is confined to bed. In spite of the title, there is no trace of distress or self-pity in the preface — it is a jaunty and cheerful autobiographical piece, written in what he himself describes as 'a tone of levity'. Galt was physically handicapped but undefeated.

He had difficulties with walking; none with writing. A considerable number of his letters and manuscripts written from 1834 survive. Till within a few weeks of his death in early 1839, they revert to the firm penmanship he had learned as a youth in the Greenock Custom House. The manuscript in 'beautiful running script' which W. Roughead dated as early work was actually written in 1836, two years after the onset of his paralysis. In this last period in Greenock it was not merely his handwriting which revived. He returned to his craft with assurance, and in these final years of Indian summer wrote a small group of new Tales of the West, some of novella length, that rank among his best work.

Even while he was writing his *Literary Life* in London in early 1834 and planning his move to Scotland, he had not ceased his magazine contributions. Cochrane and McCrone took over the *Monthly Magazine* at the beginning of the year and this led to the appearance of poems and a review by Galt in the four issues of January to April. Lady Blessington published some of his verse in her 1834 annual, *The Book of Beauty*. *Fraser's Magazine* in August published a magnificent sketch entitled 'The Mem, or Schoolmistress. From the Papers of the Late Rev. Micah Balwhither, of Dalmailing'. This admirable study of Miss Peerie, the village schoolmistress, an extension of the *Annals of the Parish*, Galt must have submitted to *Fraser's Magazine* in July, shortly before he left Edinburgh for Greenock, when his thoughts were once more turning to the west country of his earlier success. It is a fitting prelude to his final series of stories.

2

Galt's first plan when he settled in Greenock was to continue with contributions to Maga. He offered the beginning of a four-part series on 31 December and followed this up with a 'poetical hoax' and on 25 February 1835 'a dramatical sketch'. Nothing of this was used and all Galt's later overtures were ignored. The 'young Blackwoods' sent Galt a free copy of Maga each month, but they were displeased at being saddled with the *Literary Life and Miscellanies*. Like Moir, they regarded Galt as finished, and had no intention of printing any further offerings. Galt had to look elsewhere; and during the early part of 1835 he got again in touch with their father's old rival, William Tait.

His first approach was on 9 February 1835, when he wrote requesting the name of the writer of the 'very agreeable review' of his *Autobiography*[2] — 'at the time it appeared I was too ill to request the name of the author'. Since Galt did not retain Tait's replies, it is not possible to determine if the publisher disclosed Mrs Johnstone's hand and the position she had now attained in the magazine. Galt continued to make his later offers of material to Tait, unaware perhaps that Mrs Johnstone was now fully responsible for the contents of the magazine.

Mrs Johnstone had retained her deep interest in Galt. Indeed she had begun to print in her magazine one of her own novels, 'West Country Exclusives', on a theme she derived from him — the contrast between the English-speaking genteel Scots of the East and the 'vulgar' Scots of the West. The first part of her novel appeared anonymously in the issue of October 1834. It was completed in the issues of May, June and September 1835. The

main dialect-speaking character, Bailie Pirdiddie, is based openly
on Sir Andrew Wylie and Provost Pawkie. When Mrs Johnstone
came to print the June instalment of her novel, her involvement
with Galt was now so close that one of her characters, Lady Di,
is made to comment on the self-possessed and forthright Bailie:
'Who is — pray, who is that extraordinary person — so like one's
notion of a character walked out of Galt's books?' The ensuing
dialogue in *Tait's Edinburgh Magazine*, June 1835, Mrs Johnstone's spirited defence of Galt, merits quotation in full:

> 'Exactly one of Galt's vulgar, *outré* characters', returned
> Mrs Luke, flurried, and altogether much alarmed at the pro-
> posal made by a lady who valued her own amusement before
> all the proprieties and decorums in the world, and who for the
> feelings of others entertained no more consideration than be-
> came her privileged birth and high-toned manners.
>   'I know *you* detest vulgarity', rejoined Lady Di; 'but *we*
> enjoy it of all things — or a spice of it, now and then — and
> Galt —'
>   'Don't name him, Lady Di. I assure you his broad vulgarity
> and caricature is abominated in Scotland in anything approach-
> ing good society.'
>   '*Chaque un a son gout*, my dear ma'am', said Lady Di,
> shrugging her shoulders; 'there is a certain Girzy Hipple that
> almost killed me with laughing, and whom Byron absolutely
> adored.'
>   'Byron! Lord Byron?' cried the amazed Mrs Luke. It was
> altogether beyond her comprehension that Mrs Walkinshaw,
> that vulgarest of all vulgar characters, should be relished by
> Lord Byron.
>   'Have you ever had the fecility of meeting the original, my
> dear Mrs Luke? I should have gone a hundred miles to see her.'
>   Mrs Luke was fairly posed whether to plead guilty to the
> ignorance, or to deny the vulgar contamination. Her answer
> was equivocal: 'I have seen abundant oddities and vulgar
> people in Scotland; — in manners, you are aware, Lady Di, our
> home-bred people are terribly behind.'
>   'O dear! and so they are; but I have a fancy for vulgarians —
> now I know *you* can't abide them — so much for difference of
> taste. You remember Goldsmith's showman, Rugby?'
>   The Colonel was startled from a long fit of rumination, a
> most unusual observance of taciturnity.

'No, 'pon honour, I don't, Lady Di — just at this moment, at any rate.'

'A most unwonted and supererogatory degree of candour in an Irishman, who knows everything and at all times. But what has come over you? — Goldsmith's showman, you remember, detested everything *low*, and never allowed his bear to dance to any but the genteelest of tunes, as "*Water parted*", or the "*Minuet in Ariadne*".'

Mrs Luke, feeling the palpable insult, could not even join in the loud laugh which the Colonel forced up.

It is difficult to see how this remarkable passage of combined narrative and critical commentary could have been written merely from a reading of Galt's published works, so much of it is Galt's own. The term *outré*, in particular, is derived from Galt's private critical vocabulary; he uses it of his odd characters in his letters, once in his *Literary Life*. Either directly as editor or, more probably, through William Tait as the ostensible editor, Mrs Johnstone had established contact with Galt in Greenock. In 'West Country Exclusives' she publicly rallies to the defence of Galt, whose outspoken 'The Howdie' she had already published, to the disquiet of the Maga group. The discomfiture of Mrs Luke in 'West Country Exclusives' is a not too gentle hit at Blackwood's favoured Susan Ferrier, the author of *Marriage*, who had already pronounced *her* judgment on Galt — 'I have not read *Sir Andrew Wylie*, as I can't endure that man's writings, and I'm told the vulgarity of this beats print'.[3] It is hardly surprising that Galt's best work thereafter appeared in *Tait's Edinburgh Magazine*, under the approving editorship of Mrs Johnstone.

While the new owners of *Blackwood's Magazine* cold-shouldered Galt, *Fraser's Magazine* continued to give him a place of honour. The issue of January 1835 opened with an engraving of 'The Fraserians' and Maclise's drawing shows Galt sitting in the 'back room' of 215 Regent Street in the distinguished company of a group that included Carlyle, Coleridge and Thackeray. With this support, Galt in the early months of 1835 set himself solidly to a variety of tasks. His old friend, Lady Blessington, published a new novel, *The Two Friends*, in February. Galt wrote a long review, and sent her a copy on 24 March.[4] His intention was that the review would be signed. It is likely, however, to be the review

which appeared unsigned in the April issue of *Fraser's Magazine*,
where *A Quintette of Novels* was reviewed. Maginn in his intro-
ductory remarks announced that he had sent a batch of novels for
review to a group of 'the most eminent hands in our literature'.
When he received the separate reviews he printed them, with an
introduction and linking passages of his own, in the form of one
long anonymous article.

Perhaps as a result of this, Galt's next contribution, in the May
issue, was a signed article, 'Anonymous Publications', an appeal
against 'the abuse of the liberty of the press'. Galt comes out
strongly against unsigned reviews — 'It argues the possession of a
mean and cowardly spirit to stab in the dark . . . writers in that
walk of literature no longer endeavour to give a true estimate of
the work which they review, but seek to make it a peg to hang
their own wit and cleverness upon'.

Alongside these pieces of vigorous and assured journalism,
(which show no sign of a failing talent) Galt was working on a
new group of stories. His first was designed for *Tait's Edinburgh
Magazine*. But, craftsman as he was, he was not satisfied with its
shape — 'the "Elder" I thought of', he wrote Tait, 'cannot yet
be written not having found a right mode'.[5] He turned instead to
a more straightforward story for *Fraser's Magazine*, 'The Metro-
politan Emigrant', which was printed in the September issue.
This lively short story is a sort of inverted version of *Lawrie Todd*.
Mr Needles, the London haberdasher, sets up a store in Canada
and in a sequence of serio-comic episodes finds that neither he nor
his wife are the stuff of which settlers are made; and he returns to
London to be 're-established in a shop, into which I was right
glad to enter', finished for ever with 'the folly of emigration'.
Galt could still write with humorous irony.

One other story in *Fraser's Magazine* in 1835 I assign to Galt
— the case for the attribution is more fully set out in the Appendix.
The unsigned 'The Jordans of Grange and the Old Maids of
Balmogy' in the July issue is a well-constructed story, set in a
Scottish village and written in Galt's west-country dialect. Two
harsh maiden sisters adopt their orphaned nephew, and engage
another orphan, Mary Ballantyne, as a servant. The two young
people fall in love and the girl has a child — a 'bastard bairn', in
the forthright language of the unnamed author. The sisters

separate the lovers and take over the baby. Years later Mary returns a rich widow and is reunited to her ill-used child and separated lover.

In the manner of *The Ayrshire Legatees*, the village dialect voices comment bluntly, in the person of Nanze Hadie, the fish-wife — 'I serv'd your cankered father, that's dead and awa'; and I serv'd your genty sister, the best o' the whole o' ye, whose heart ye broke amang you, because it wasna as hard as your ain; and now ye are doing your best to break twa young hearts, that the north blasts o' the world has driven under your lee, because they committed a natural misbehave, that auld maids should say extraordinar little about. I red me it would be lang to the day or the likes o' *you* would fa' into a curcudeugh wi' a bonnie lad. Deil a bit that I should say it, ye ne'er were ony temptation, for a' your gear.' This is the very language and rhetoric of 'the Leddy', *aut Galt aut diabolus.*

The contributions to *Fraser's Magazine* did not exhaust Galt's list of productions for 1835. He wrote to Tait on 22 August, apologizing for not having completed the promised 'Elder' — but he has 'compleated another story "Tribulations" . . . it is after the manner of the Annals of the Parish. . . . It is an odd but common trait of incidents and derives its interest from being written as an autobiographer's memoir . . .' Tait may have the 'pre-emption' of the copyright since Galt plans republication in volume form.[6] The issues of November and December 1835 and January 1836 of *Tait's Edinburgh Magazine* duly printed the novella-length 'Tribulations of the Rev. Conal Kilmun'. Mrs Johnstone firmly announced it as 'By John Galt'. After her open defence of Galt in 'West Country Exclusives', the anonymity of 'The Howdie' was no longer called for.

'Tribulations', in spite of Galt's description, is not after the manner of *Annals of the Parish*. It is a strange, oddly-powerful and surrealistic tale. The Rev. Conal Kilmun is the pastor of a small village on the shores of a sea-loch of the Clyde. Into his life — they simply arrive 'over the ferry' — come two mysterious figures, Mr Ettles (once a young man of the parish) and his companion Mr Roslin. The minister becomes over the years involved with them. A message of distress from Roslin causes him to cross over the ferry to his aid, only to be present at his unexplained death and to receive, as a tribute to his own 'apostolic simplicity', a valuable legacy. Ettles then summons him to Edinburgh to receive the legacy; and the minister, who had hitherto known only the pious and formal Edinburgh of the General Assembly of the Church, is conducted on a phantasmagoric tour of poverty and prostitution in the 'dens of depravity and hiding-places of wo' of the city's underworld among the 'closes and unsavoury nooks of the Cowgate, as well as all the Canongate'. 'Sorrowful unto a sickness of the heart' the ministers leaves 'yon abominable corners of Edinburgh' for the quiet of his parish.

This disturbing tale, for all its loose ends and unexplained incidents (its 'odd but common train of incidents'), is strangely successful. There is a blend of brooding mystery and sharp realism. The phantasmagoria of the Edinburgh slum scenes foreshadows 'Tom-all-Alone's' in the London of *Bleak House* and the 'Night-Town' of James Joyce's Dublin. 'Tribulations' has a symbolic and parable quality that Galt was possibly not himself entirely aware of. He had abandoned his ambitions for a life of action — to 'ettle' is to 'strive'[7] — and the tale is a commentary on the temptation and corruption that lie 'over the ferry'. Like 'The Howdie' it could have found no place in the self-satisfied world of *Blackwood's Magazine*, and it took Mrs Johnstone to see its quality.

3

While 'Tribulations' was appearing in *Tait's Edinburgh Magazine*, Galt wrote a section of another story and on 13 December 1835 offered it to the Blackwoods. They were not interested. There is no way of identifying the offering — Galt merely calls it 'the inclosed fiction'. It was possibly the opening pages of 'A Rich Man'. But its composition that month shows Galt still hard at work. Early in the following year, on 26 February, he offered a further article 'as a gratuitous contribution'. This too was refused, and Galt replied on 12 March 'I presume from various circumstances that it is not desired I should continue a contributor to the magazine' — and, in the circumstances, he declined to 'receive the publication gratuitously'.

His copies of Maga continued to arrive. But Galt once again

knew he had to look elsewhere. *Fraser's Magazine* in January
1836 opened with a mock Parliamentary Report on the conduct
of the magazine and in this triumphant article Galt found himself
included among 'the leading lights of literature'. This was more
heartening than a free copy of Maga. Galt had always as a spare-
time activity tinkered with mechanical devices, from Aeolian
harps to arrangements of pulleys, and in a letter to Lockhart post-
marked 4 January 1836[8] he mentioned a 'paper about my Seafed
Engine'. The dependable *Fraser's Magazine* printed in the April
issue his signed descriptive article, 'On the Sea-Fed Engine, for
propelling Vessels instead of Steam'. Galt took his plan seriously,
but his knowledge of physics and mechanics was elementary — he
admits he is 'only a dabbler in principles' and apologetically calls
himself 'Old Philosophorum' — and the paper was no more than
an easy money-spinner exploiting one of his hobbies.

The refusal of proffered articles was not the only shock contained in the Blackwoods' letter of 10 March. There was also a
request for repayment of the advance made by their father against
the future profits of the *Literary Life and Miscellanies*. There had
been no profits, and Galt was consequently in debt to the firm to
the tune of £250. He could not pay. Galt in early 1836 not
merely had no money; he was living on borrowings. Too honourable a man of business to evade his obligations, he wrote back on
12 March requesting that they charge him interest on the debt
till it could be liquidated, and (much against the grain) gave a
brief explanation of his unexpected financial predicament.

None of his friends knew that he was in sore straits. Even two
years after his death, Moir in the *Memoir* recorded that 'it was
only recently that most of them, and myself among the rest', were
able to learn of Galt's actual situation in retirement. There was
only one friend to whom he could bring himself to make a full
disclosure, Lockhart, the one literary man who had subscribed to
his *Literary Life*. In two letters, of 4 January and 28 March,[9]
Galt gave Lockhart in considerable detail the 'curious secret
history' of his finances.

It had been assumed by all that Galt in 1834 had retired to
Scotland on an adequate competency, supplemented by a government pension. Galt at first thought so himself; either because he
was ill or possibly through sheer quixotic pride, when he left

London he had even refused a cash grant proposed by the Directors of the British American Land Company. He unburdened himself to Lockhart of the whole story: the pension had turned out to be no pension, simply a single payment of £200, recommended by the King; his wife's annuity from her shares in *The Star* had vanished, when the executor of Dr Tilloch's estate failed; meanwhile (under the terms of Dr Tilloch's somewhat tortuous will)[10] the trustees could pay no other income from the estate till Alexander turned twenty-one in three years' time; Galt's sons, though they had the previous year been given a government grant of land in Canada, were looking for cash to develop their property; and there was no income from Galt's last book, only a debt of £250 plus interest. Galt had nothing. 'In fact had I not done an act of justice to my sister many years ago when my hopes were perhaps different, I would be in absolute beggary' — she had made over to him half her income and had advanced to Galt and his sons over a thousand pounds.

It is no wonder that he found the Blackwoods' request for repayment a shock — 'I am obliged', he wrote them, 'to subsist on borrowed money'. To Lockhart he was more forthright — 'this matter of the Blackwoods for which I had thought they had done something to remedy the effects of their negligence is the feather which has broken the stout back, and forced me thus to address you'. His letters to Lockhart are an appeal for help, not for money, but for some kind of commendation — 'I really require a lift now to revive my book' — which he calls quite frankly a 'pot boiler'. In the second letter, he sent Lockhart 'two little works' (one of them his recent volume of poems) in the hope that Lockhart would review them — 'I think by Fraser you could do me some good now'. Lockhart's side of the correspondence has disappeared — Galt kept few letters — but it was clearly friendly in tone. Galt was pleased at Lockhart's 'strong feeling under the surface of much prudence', his 'flow under what others may think ice'. There is no trace of a review by Lockhart. But Galt secured a commission from Henry Colburn to edit a four volume *Diary illustrative of the Times of George the Fourth*, which ultimately appeared in 1838 and 1839 with a firm and well-written preface and a publisher's postscript on the 'distinguished person who edited these volumes'. Lockhart had secured for Galt in 1830 the

opportunity to write for Colburn the *Lives of the Players*, and
this new commission is likely to have been a further and timely
gesture of friendship.

4

If *Blackwood's Magazine* would not publish his work, Galt knew
where to turn. On 4 January 1836 he offered Tait the copyright
of his old 1823 manuscript, the life of William Paterson.[11] It
found no favour with Tait or Mrs Johnstone. They were hoping
for a continuation 'in the peculiar style' of his recent stories, and
Galt promptly on 17 January replied to Tait that the Scottish
story he had 'just finished I think my best. It is the autobiography
of a "man or merit" the late Archd. Plack'.[12] If (as is likely) it is
'the inclosed fiction' which the Blackwoods had rejected a few
weeks earlier, Maga had lost heavily. Mrs Johnstone printed it in
the June, July and August issues of *Tait's Edinburgh Magazine*
with a massive displayed title, 'A Rich Man; or He has Great
Merit. Being the Autobiography of Archibald Plack, Esq., Late
Lord Mayor of London, In a series of letters to his grandson, the
Honourable George Spend. By John Galt'.

  'A Rich Man', written throughout in west-country dialect, is
Galt at his ironic best. Plack, now a wealthy old man, has had a
letter from his Oxford undergraduate grandson 'anent replenish-
ments'. But 'riches arc no gatherit like sclate stanes' and he tells
his 'oe and heir' his own life-story. He was left 'an orphan with
an old aunty' and having 'perfitted my edication' at the age of
eight hills for three years a 'vacuity in the druggist's shop' and
then decides 'to spouse my fortune as an errander in Glasgow'.
He saves money as an errand boy and wins through 'with an
ettle'. Moving on one of his errands to Liverpool he meets an
Irishman who instals him in a warehouse in London and so 'I was
led cannily into the provision line'. He lends a man a pound, and
a guinea is duly returned, 'so, littles by littles, I creepit into the
banking line'. A prudent marriage follows and the death of his
wife. 'Seeing myself, by the blessing of God, and the removal of
my wife, in a state of mair business than I ever thought to be in,
I again began to think how I could best cast my bread upon the
waters'. He thrives by lending and shrewd dealing — 'the Lord

aye prospers the well-doing with prosperity' — remarries and
inherits from his father-in-law a substantial sum — 'there's no
endowment in nature equal to the dripping roast of a fat legacy'.

With prosperity came honours. He becomes sheriff, alderman,
and finally Lord Mayor — Lord Mayors being 'a wee sort of
nobility for the remainder of their days'. The last section is a
typical Galt finale — the triumphal 'jaunt' of the Plack family
back to Glasgow — 'Everybody kens it is as natural for a Scotchman, who has done well in the world, to show his testimonies
among his kith and kin when he grows old, as it is for him to eat
parritch for his breakfast, and to go about barefooted when
young'. Daughter Clemy, having been sent to boarding school 'to
learn manners, and to play on the spinnet' marries a young lord.
Plack [no Walter Scott] cannily refuses a baronetcy — the fees
were too dear — 'I thought it a concos mentos job to pay for a
nickname' — and pawkily enclosing the required 'replenishment'
in his final letter assures his grandson that 'those upon the thrive
have great merit; but to know what to do with money is the craft
of life'.

Galt in this excellent story combines all the elements that had
always made up his strength as a novelist, the ironical self-
revelation of the narrator, the exploitation of the resources of
dialect (the story is inconceivable in English), the counterpointing
of eighteenth-century Scottish small-town life with the wider
world of business and of public affairs in London, the shrewd
understanding of the manipulations and power politics of a hero
who is at the same time kindly and human and yet assiduously
'upon the thrive'. 'A Rich Man', the last major story by Galt, is a
distillation of the best of his earlier writing.

While his mind was still on the theme, he wrote a further
sketch. It appeared in the December issue of *Fraser's Magazine*,
'The Statesman. By John Galt'. It is a parallel career, written in
English, not Scots. The Prime Minister, 'having attained my
grand climacteric' and scenting that the administration is losing
ground, retires to write not his memoirs but 'a treatise on the
principles by which states may be ruled best'. Galt's old reading
of Machiavelli and his memory of years of lobbying in the House
of Commons produces an ironic — even cynical — manual on
how to rise from Member of Parliament (attract attention by

'moving from seat to seat during the stillness of a solemn debate' and look as if you had 'secrets to whisper to many men'), to Under-Secretary of State ('the rulers of the state, and their superiors but superintendents'), to Secretary of State ('their chief duty is to keep themselves from being mixed up with transactions, the issue of which is uncertain'), and finally to the full manipulative power of the Prime Ministership. 'The Statesman' is a tightly-written and witty variation on one of Galt's favourite themes.

With this Parthian shot, Galt rounded off his effective writing career. *Fraser's Magazine* and *Tait's Edinburgh Magazine* had given him a fresh lease of life. It was now the close of 1836; he still had a few more years to go; he would continue, as was his wont, to put pen to paper; but the Indian summer was over. It had lasted a little over two years and it had added a few small masterpieces written by the real John Galt.

11. Epilogue

1

'I THOUGHT myself growing better, and endeavoured to renew my usual activity', Galt wrote later of the years 1835 and 1836, 'it was not strength but a spasm.'[1] Paralysis clamped down again, this time finally, and he knew that his real work was over.

These final years are more fully documented than many more important periods in his life — he was haunted in 1838 by a literary lady, Miss Harriet Pigott, who was determined to write his life. She importuned the ageing and reluctant author for his reminiscences and collected information from two associates in Greenock. Her manuscript gatherings — letters from Galt and his wife, the recollections of Alexander Rodger and G. J. Weir, and her own brief pietistic biography — were left to the Bodleian. It is a disappointing collection. None of the contributors had known Galt during his days of activity and vigour. None of them was in his confidence, as William Blackwood and Dr Moir and J. G. Lockhart had been — indeed G. J. Weir, with frank honesty, claimed only a recent and 'coffee-room or library acquaintance'. None of them knew that privately in letters to Edinburgh he was calling Greenock a 'one-eyed' and 'a stupid' place. Patiently putting up with his disabilities and his reduced way of life and fully conscious that his creative fires had died, Galt in his mind re-lived quietly the years of his bustling activity in a bigger world.

Yet he continued with at least the mechanics of writing. He was unable to drop the habit. He published a long autobiographical letter in the July 1837 issue of *Fraser's Magazine*, setting firmly to rights some published inaccuracies about his career. He turned over and revised his old manuscripts. The editing of the *Diary Illustrative of the Times of George the Fouth* remained a satisfactory stand-by, the first two volumes appearing in 1838 and the

final two, shortly after his death, in 1839. He kept up a correspondence with his sons, delighted that they had fought on the
government side during the Rebellion in Canada. He wrote to old
friends, including the long-forgiven Dr Valpy and the industrious
Lady Blessington. He continued to harass the 'young Blackwoods'. He even offered them on 1 February 1837 a *fourth*
volume of the *Literary Life and Miscellanies*, to revive the sale of
the other three. There is no record of the reply. A year later he
came at them again. Having had another look at his old papers,
he proposed on 4 January 1838 that they could publish 'a number
of sketches' as a volume to be entitled *Clishmaclavers*. The only
response was his free copy of Maga. Galt was too spent in body
and mind to write anything new, and no one wanted his old
savings. A few of the prose sketches and a volume of verse found
their way into print after his death.

   In his final months two public tributes came his way. His old
friend and physician in London, Dr A. T. Thomson, took it upon
himself in June 1838 to make an application to the Literary
Fund, and Galt was awarded a grant of £50.[2] The Watt Club of
Greenock decided to have his portrait painted and Galt made his
last public appearance on 20 January 1839 on the occasion of
the unveiling. As a one-time haunter of artist's studios, he was
pleased. It was not the first time, since he became a public figure,
that he had sat for an artist. Maclise had done a line-drawing for
Fraser's Magazine in 1830; William Blackwood in a letter of
January 1833 had proclaimed that everyone was delighted with
his recent 'Miniature'; for the *Autobiography* Galt had an engraving made in 1833 at the cost of 'about £40'; there is mention
the same year of 'my own medallion'; a black and white drawing
dated March 1834 hangs in the National Portrait Gallery in
London; and he was painted in July 1835 for a portrait now in
the Scottish National Portrait Gallery in Edinburgh. Galt was
delighted at the new honour of another portrait provided by his
fellow citizens but — living in his private dream of an active past
elsewhere — insisted that the artist paint him as he had looked
ten years earlier.

   He died, after a brief illness, on 11 April 1839.[3] There were
several obituaries, the most appreciative (for all its many inaccuracies) appearing in the July *Gentleman's Magazine*. It is a

warm tribute to 'a most intelligent and agreeable companion. . . .
The public will not soon forget his "Ayrshire Legatees", his
"Annals of the Parish" nor "The Entail", which last we think
one of his best novels'. His wife Elizabeth wrote Miss Pigott on
24 May expressing 'the pleasure your visits afforded to one now
no more and very dear to me'. She was due in a few days to sail,
with her husband's old papers,[4] to join Alick in Canada.

'He has left', wrote the *Gentleman's Magazine*, 'his widow and
family struggling with adverse circumstances'. It was a reasonable
assumption, particularly if word had got around of Dr Thomson's
application to the Literary Fund. It was not, in fact, true. Galt's
brave fight on a variety of fronts had benefited everyone. The
grant of 1200 acres of land in Canada which the government
belatedly made him in 1838 he had divided among his sons, to
add to their own grants. Mrs Galt was able to write after a year
in Canada that she was 'in the enjoyment of every comfort'. She
was back again in London and Scotland for the years 1842–3,
when Alick came to advise his Directors. She returned with him
to Canada, when he was appointed Secretary of the Company.
Her eldest son, John, would become a senior official of the
Canada Company. Tom would become Sir Thomas Galt, Knight
Bachelor, and a Chief Justice. Alick would become a wealthy
man, Minister of Finance, first Canadian High Commissioner in
London, and in the fullness of time Sir Alexander Tilloch Galt,
Knight Grand Cross of the Order of St Michael and St George.
The 'young Blackwoods' would assemble all the Galt copyrights
which their father had purchased and have Dr Moir edit them in
1841–2 in four volumes of Blackwood's Standard Novels. In that
format they commanded a steady sale throughout the nineteenth
century until they were supplanted in 1895 by a re-issue entitled
'Works of John Galt'. Galt could rest quietly in Greenock. His
family was secure; his literary reputation was secure; his books
were selling; and — to a man of his sense of business punctilio it
would have mattered — he had paid off that £250.

2

Today what Galt most needs is a fresh judgment, and available
texts. He has never lacked admirers or appreciative critics. The

four volumes of the 'Blackwood' novels, forming the 'Works of John Galt' have in the past been seen as admirable 'secondary Scottish novels'; as regional novels; as dialect comedy of a high order; as documentation of the social history of Scotland. They are all of these, but none is an adequate judgment on his full achievement. Galt has in the past tended to attract not so much serious critics as devotees.

In recent years, Galt criticism has taken a new turn. He is being regarded as a more serious writer than earlier readers had ever conceived him to be, a man of the Enlightenment, sensitive to the major economic and intellectual issues of his day, and yet the best and most sympathetic interpreter in fiction of Scottish calvinism; a philosophic sceptic conditioned by Adam Smith and Adam Ferguson whose major works can be read as part of the indigenous Scottish philosophy of his time; *The Entail* has been subjected to the rigours of an analysis based on Aristotle's critical insights; *The Provost* has been examined as an exercise in political thought stemming from Machiavelli. These are moves in the right direction. Galt is more than a superb dialect entertainer. He is a novelist of real originality.

Several factors have made proper criticism of Galt difficult. His photographic realism can itself be a snare for the reader. It is all so clear, so accurate, so Wilkie-like in its period detail. We accept it (as Blackwood's old mother did) *as* real. We tend to agree unthinkingly with Christopher North that *Annals of the Parish* is not a book but a fact. It is not, however; it *is* a novel, a highly-skilled literary artefact; behind it all Galt the artificer, selecting, interpreting, manipulating character and incident with a unique blend of affection and irony, offering by implication in his picture of the small world a commentary on the impact of changing ideas in the larger world, and a humane and decent gloss on the human situation everywhere. Galt's art conceals itself.

A second difficulty has been the sheer bulk of his output. Galt wrote too much. The volume of what he had to write has always masked the importance and even the existence of the work he really wanted to write. Only by establishing, as the present study has attempted, the circumstances that lay behind each of his writings, and so isolating the man who wrote 'con amore' from

the merely enforced writer, is it possible to distinguish the corpus
of work on which he himself wished to be judged and on which
he should be judged. Galt himself, once the evidence is examined,
never leaves us in doubt.

A further complication lies in his relationship with his publishers, particularly with William Blackwood. The partnership of
Blackwood and Galt was critical. It came at the right time in
Galt's career. Without William Blackwood, it is highly probable
that Galt would never have emerged as a novelist of significance.
The encouragement, and the acceptance by *Blackwood's Magazine* of *The Ayrshire Legatees* was the turning point. But Galt
outgrew Blackwood and the restricted range of sensibilities of the
Maga circle, and the association came to inhibit him. Blackwood
affected adversely the shape of several of the novels, then censored
to extinction *The Last of the Lairds*, and in the end was not even
given the offer of the best of Galt's later work.

The well-intended pressures of the Blackwood group ultimately
had a distorting effect on Galt's reputation, limiting his appeal in
a manner of which few readers can be conscious. The Galt works
that have always been readily available have been those — and
only those — that bore the stamp of Blackwood's approval. Only
the Blackwood copyrights have remained continuously in print.
Opinion has swung from time to time on the relative merits of
The Entail, The Provost, and *Annals of the Parish,* but these
have always been the basis for all but the rarest appreciation of
Galt. There has, as a consequence of this printing history, always
been an unconscious assumption that anything not in print —
anything, that is, other than Blackwood's approved choices —
could be safely ignored, as part of Galt's massive hack-work, not
worthy of reprinting.

For a full assessment, the Galt works that Blackwood suppressed or ignored must be brought into the corpus of his work.
They will not displace the best of the Blackwood titles, but their
addition will present a fuller and more accurate picture of a
serious novelist who had much more to offer than the comedy of
Scottish village life. The downright *Ringan Gilhaize* (not included
in the collected 'Works of John Galt' till 1936) is an effective and
non-romantic historical novel, the work of a detached and scepti-
cal mind that could yet assess fairly the dour independent spirit of

Scottish calvinism. The later tales in *Fraser's Magazine*, notably 'The Mem' and 'The Statesman', show a Galt who can enrich earlier themes. The Galt who was accepted by *Tait's Edinburgh Magazine* goes beyond the cosy village chronicler — the earthy *The Howdie*, the rich ironies of Alexander Plack, and the disturbing horrors of the *Tribulations* have a power of imagination and insight unequalled in the better known Blackwood novels. Galt's own text of *The Last of the Lairds*, far from being the disappointing work that the Blackwood group made of it, is — as Galt intended — a work of rude vigour and a triumphant rounding-off of the *roman-fleuve*. Above all, *The Member*, unreprinted since 1832, is a pioneering and utterly original work, the beginnings of the English political novel. The retrieval, from research libraries, of the whole achievement of the real Galt, and his adequate presentation to the general reader, is an act of justice long overdue.

Appendix 1.
Galt attributions

1. *'An Autumn in the North'*

M. M. H. Thrall in her study of *Fraser's Magazine, Rebellious Fraser's* (1934) attributes to Galt the authorship of an unsigned series 'An Autumn in the North' that appeared in the magazine October 1834–February 1835. It is an account of a visit to Scotland in 'The Monarch', the Leith steam packet by which Galt travelled in June 1834. The writer then describes a visit to Stirling and Loch Lomond, shows great familiarity with fishing and shooting, proclaims himself an Anglican, attends an episcopalian service at Stirling, and is acutely critical of presbyterianism.

The attribution rests on the author's assumption that a statement ['G—'s Autumn in the North . . . a vile calumny on the country of his birth'], in a letter cited in Moir's life of Robert MacNish prefaced to the latter's collection *The Modern Pythagorean* of 1838, refers to Galt. But the details of the trip do not correspond with Galt's movements of 1834, and the sporting interests and aggressive Anglican attitude are quite alien to him. G— is unquestionably, not Galt, but a different Fraserian, the Rev. G. R. Gleig, novelist, Anglican clergyman, ex-soldier, a regular visitor to Scotland for fishing and shooting, and the son of the episcopalian Bishop of Stirling. He was written up in the 'Gallery of Literary Characters' in *Fraser's Magazine* of September 1834 as 'now enjoying his thirtieth season of the moors', of which 'An Autumn in the North' was the outcome.

2. *'The Jordans of Grange and the Old Maids of Balmogy'*

This anonymous story was printed in Fraser's Magazine, July 1835, with the sub-title 'A Tradition of the Dominie'. I have found no external evidence for its authorship. The internal signs that point to Galt as the author are:

1. The 'rhythm' of the title, for which Galt's known works show parallels.
2. The subtitle, cf. Galt's sub-title 'A Tradition of the Backwoods' in *Fraser's Magazine*, October 1830.
3. The character of the 'Old maid' sisters, cf. the 'old maid' sisters of Barenbraes in *The Last of the Lairds*.
4. The detailed description of women's costume, particularly the 'old-fashioned' constume of elderly ladies, cf. *The Entail*.

145

5. The place-name 'Balmogy', cf. 'Mrs Ogle of Balbogle', *Blackwood's Magazine*, October 1821.
6. The use of many of Galt's 'characteristic' terms, e.g. 'gentry', 'gear', 'wastery', 'fashery'; 'improvements' (cf. *The Entail*); 'bastard bairn' (cf. 'The Howdie').
7. The 'labelling' of characters — Mr Doitre, the elderly clergyman; Nanze Hadie, the fishwife; Mr Stircup, the inn-keeper.
8. The long-rhetorical expostulations by Nanze Hadie, cf. 'The Leddy' in *The Entail*.
9. The consistent and precisely accurate west country dialect. None of the known 'Fraserians' who could write Scots dialect stories [Lockhart, Hogg, Gleig, Moir] write in this dialect.
10. The story is written by a skilled hand. One can eliminate any known beginner. Of the known writers of Scots stories of the period, Galt seems the only candidate.

Appendix 2.

Oliver & Boyd's stock-sheets 1825

Oliver and Boyd, in response to a request by Galt of 18 August 1825 for a report on the sales of his books, supplied him with a list, and retained the following copy:

Stock 18th August 1825.

ROTHELAN No. 2000
240 copies qrs.
 39   Do bds.
 ___
279 copies
 ___
 25   „   Simpkin

SPAEWIFE No. 3000
373 copies quires
 37 Do   bds.
 ___
400 Copies
 ___

RINGAN No. 3000
860 Copies qrs.
 45   „   bds.
 ___
905
 ___
 12 Simpkin

BACHELOR'S WIFE No. 2000
198 Copies qrs.
105   „   bds.
 ___
303
 ___
 25 Simpkin

Wolsey
69 qrs.
5 bds.
———
74 Copies
———
Whittaker.

[Oliver and Boyd, after the date of my examination of their material, have transferred it to the National Library of Scotland.]

Appendix 3.

The subscribers to Galt's 'Literary Life and Miscellanies'

The following list of subscribers is transcribed from two copies of a broadsheet prospectus, now part of N.L.S. MS. 4038. One copy has additional names in Galt's hand.

Subscribers' Names and Residences, with numbers of Copies subscribed for.

The Marquess of Breadalbane.
The Marquess of Sligo, K.P.
The Right Honourable Edward Ehce.
James Ewing, Esq. M.P. Glasgow.
Kirkman Finlay, Esq. (six copies.)
James Finlay, Esq. (two copies.)
John Finlay, Esq. (two copies.)
James Beuborrow, (two copies.)
John Hodgson, Esq. St. Helen's Place, London.
Hugh Matthie, Esq. Liverpool.
Alexander Dunlop, Esq. Keppoch, Dumbartonshire.
George Clarke Cheape, Esq.
D. C. Guthrie, Esq. Idol Lane, London.
The Lord Provost of Glasgow.
Alex. Dunlop, Esq. Advocate, Glasgow. (five copies.)
James Walker, Esq. Gt. George Street. (two copies.)
John Gibson Lockhart, Esq. Regent's Park.
John May, Esq. Glasgow.
His Grace the Duke of Wellington.
Boyd Miller, Esq. (ten copies.)
Sir James Shaw, Bart. (fourteen copies.)
Lord Willoughby D'Ersby.

Lady Willoughby D'Ersby.
James Dunlop, Esq. Russell Square.
Major Yule.
George Yule, Esq.
The Countess of Blessington.
Count D'Orsay.
M. Stanley, Esq.
Lord Abercromby.
The Honourable Fox Maul.
Roger Aytoun, Esq. W. S. Edinburgh.
Robert Rutherford, Esq. W. S. Edinburgh.
Thomas Johnson, Esq. Edinburgh.
Patrick Mackenzie, Esq. W. S. Edinburgh.
Robert McFarlane, Esq. W. S. Edinburgh.
James McFarlane, Esq. W. S. Edinburgh.
Dr Maclagan, Edinburgh.
Peter Lang, Esq. Edinburgh.
Archibald Gibson, Esq. Edinburgh.
——Rae, Esq. Edinburgh.
George Hewitt, Esq. Edinburgh.
Peter Forbes, Esq. Edinburgh.
William Pollock, Esq. Edinburgh.
William Brooks, Esq. Lasswade.
Arthur Megett, Esq. Edinburgh.

Charles Neaves, Esq. Advocate, Edinburgh.
W. K. Hunter, Esq. Dunse.
John Spence, Esq. Edinburgh.
John Macfie, Esq. Edinburgh.
John Macnair, Esq. Edinburgh.
Marquess of Londonderry.
Viscount Castlereagh.
Lord Gardner.
General the Honourable E. Phipps.
General Sir Robert Wilson.
Roland Errington, Esq.
Walter Little Gilmore, Esq.
Viscount Ossulstone.
Lord Elphinstone.
Honourable J. Ponsonby.
Professor Dr. A. T. Thomson.
Sir John Key.
Viscount Allen.
Richard Williams, Esq.
Mrs. R. Macfie.
Mrs. James Dunlop.
William Steuart, Esq.
Lady Halliday.
Messrs. William Smith and Son, Liverpool.
Hugh Matthie, Esq. Liverpool.
John Eason, Esq. Liverpool.
Alexander Gibb, Esq. Liverpool.
Hugh Craig, Esq. Liverpool.

John W. Buchanan, Esq. Liverpool.
John Wilson, Esq. Liverpool.
Alexander McGregor, Esq. Liverpool.
Alexander Reid, Esq. Liverpool.
David Craig, Esq. Liverpool.
Archibald Robinson, Esq. Liverpool.
Hudson Gurney, Esq. V.P.A.S. London.
Messrs. A. Service and John Ferguson, (ten copies.)
Mrs Sprot. (two copies.)
Miss Sprot. (two copies.)
H. Gouger, Esq. (two copies.)
William Miller, Esq. (two copies.)
Jonathan Chapman, Esq. (two copies.)
John Sheddan, Esq.
Major Montgomery.
John Jeffray, Esq.
Rev. G. G. S. Halton.
The Manchester Subscription Library.
Matthew Boyd, Esq. (two copies.)
William McDougall, Esq.
Alexander McDougall, Esq.
Bernard Hebelir, Esq.
George Young, Esq.
David McIntosh, Esq.

Galt has added to one printed list the following: Saml. Omay, Esq., Edinburgh; Wm. Atchison, Esq., Dromore; Hugh Moir, Esq., Musselburgh; Dr. Moir Ditto — copy from me to Delta [i.e. Galt *gave* Moir a copy]; John McGowan, Esq., Peebles. Galt's marked copy was sent to Robert Blackwood, 'annexed' to a letter of 20 August 1834, with instructions to arrange delivery. On Galt's evidence, the delivery was 'neglected'.

Notes

Chapter 2

1. Quotations from both the *Autobiography* and the *Literary Life* occur frequently in my narrative. Page references are given in the notes only where the specific reference has special significance. Where a quoted passage is not identified in the text, the source is the *Autobiography*.
2. 'Reminiscences of Some of his Contemporaries', in James Hogg, *The Poetical Works of the Ettrick Shepherd*, 1838–40, vol. v, pp. cxiv–cxv.
3. Galt (exceptionally for him) retained Park's letters. He printed them in his *Literary Life*. All Park letters quoted are from this source.
4. A. Cunningham, *Life of Sir David Wilkie*, 1843, vol. i, chaps. ii–v.
5. National Library of Scotland [N.L.S. in later references], MS. 9035, ff.15–16.
6. Galt to W. Blackwood, 5 Sept. 1832. N.L.S. MS. 4033, f. 8— 'It was sent to Wilkie before his painting on that subject was undertaking'.
7. *Literary Life*, chap. ix, prints Park's letter on the negotiations.
8. Galt's letter to Scott is in N.L.S. MS. 3833, f. 38. For Scott's reply see *Letters of Sir Walter Scott* (ed. Grierson), vol. iii, pp. 146–9.
9. Galt received Scott's letter (of 16 July 1812) in Gibraltar. He did not reply till 24 March 1813 — his letter is now in N.L.S. MS. 3884, ff. 108–9.
10. Public Record Office, PROB. II/1697 833.
11. Galt to Cadell and Davis, N.L.S. MS. 9818, ff. 156–7.
12. The draft reply is on Galt's letter. Same MS as in note 11.
13. A. Cunningham, *Life of Sir David Wilkie*, vol. i, pp. 351–3.
14. *Literary Life*, p. 152.
15. Bodleian MS. Montague d.7. f. 223.
16. Galt to Scott, N.L.S. MS. 3885, f. 251.
17. *Letters of Sir Walter Scott*, vol. iv. p. 9, where part of Galt's letter in note 16 is also printed, but the whole point of the exchange is lost since Grierson read the writer's name as 'John Gull' under which it is indexed.
18. A copy of this rare broadsheet is in N.L.S.
19. Bodleian MS. Pigott d.6.
20. Galt to Blackwood and Sons, 1 Feb. 1837. N.L.S. MS. 4044, f.228 — 'Mr Caddell purchased for £150'.
21. i.e. the total of Dr Tilloch's annuity plus his official salary.
22. Galt to Constable, 8 Dec. 1818. N.L.S. MS. 682, f.78.
23. See Joseph Priestley, *Priestley's Navigable Rivers and Canals*, 1831, pp. 266–73.
24. Constable to Galt, 11 Dec. 1818. N.L.S. MS. 790.
25. Galt to Constable, 2 Feb. 1819. N.L.S. MS. 682, f.80.
26. Constable papers in the N.L.S. MSS. 682 and 790.
27. Constable to Galt, 14 July 1819. N.L.S. MS. 790.

28. Galt to George Boyd, 6 Oct. 1823. Oliver and Boyd papers. [These, since I consulted them, have been transferred to N.L.S. Cataloguing is in process.]
29. *Pictures, Historical and Biographical*, 1821, Preface p. iii.
30. *Literary Life*, chap. xl, p. 349.

Chapter 3

1. The Galt/Blackwood letters are cited in the text by date and writer. This automatically identifies the source of the quotation, since the originals are available as follows: (a) Galt's letters to Blackwood are in the N.L.S. and are fully catalogued in National Library of Scotland, *Catalogue of Manuscripts since 1925*, vol. iii *Blackwood Papers*; (b) Copies of Blackwood's letters to Galt are in the Letter-Books of William Blackwood and Sons, 45 George Street, Edinburgh. These are not catalogued and the pagination is inadequate for reference purposes, but the letters are copied in chronological sequence. Any Galt citation is from the N.L.S. collection and any Blackwood citation is from the Letter-Books. No further identification is given in subsequent notes, unless a specific manuscript reference is required for some particular purpose.
2. cf. A. L. Strout, *A Bibliography of Articles in Blackwood's Magazine 1817–1825*, Lubbock, Texas, 1959.
3. 'C.N.' [Christopher North] in *Blackwood's Edinburgh Magazine*, June 1822, p. 744.
4. The review was reprinted (and acknowledged as Mrs Johnstone's) by D. M. Moir in his edition of *Annals of the Parish* in Blackwood's Standard Novels, 1841, pp. 308–10.
5. G. M. Trevelyan, *English Social History*, 1951 ed., vol. iii, p. 156

Chapter 4

1. Public Record Office, State Papers for Upper Canada. Several series.
2. Galt to W. Blackwood, 28 May 1821. N.L.S. MS. 4006, f.236 — 'the fasherie about them is, as Micah would say, just extraordinar'.
3. Blackwood to Maginn 23 April 1823. Blackwood Letter-Books. 'He lived with them some months while he was writing Sir Andrew Wylie'.
4. N.L.S. MS. 4005, f.245.
5. A. J. Ashley, 'Coleridge on Galt', *Times Literary Supplement*, 25 Sept. 1930, p. 757.

Chapter 5

1. Galt to Lady Blessington. Printed in *Collection of Autograph Letters and Historical Documents*, formed by Alfred Morrison, second series *The Blessington Papers*, 1895, pp. 55–6.
2. Galt to Lady Blessington. Printed in R. R. Madden, *The Literary Life and Correspondence of the Countess of Blessington*, 1885, vol. iii, p. 235.
3. *Lady Blessington's Conversations of Lord Byron*, ed. E. J. Lovell, 1969, p. 146.

4. This edition of *The Entail*, 1842, was edited by D. M. Moir for Blackwood's Standard Novels. He cites Byron's remark on p. 400.
5. These letters, examined by me in Oliver and Boyd's offices in Tweeddale Court, High Street, Edinburgh, have now been deposited in the N.L.S. They are in process of being catalogued. As with the Galt/Blackwood letters, I identify them in the text by writer and date.
6. Galt to unnamed recipient 'Dear Sir'. N.L.S. MS. 3098.
7. Blackwood to Maginn 23 April 1829. Blackwood Letter-Books.

Chapter 6

1. R. R. Madden *op. cit.*, vol. iii, p. 237.
2. Same letter.
3. Cunningham to Galt. N.L.S. MS. 621, ff.3–4.
4. Galt to William Tait, 4 Jan. 1836. N.L.S. MS. 3713, ff.74–5.
5. Scott's *Journal*, entry for 18 July 1829.
6. Bodleian MS. Pigott d.6. f.50.
7. Scott's *Journal*, entry for 23 Feb. 1826.
8. Scott's *Journal*, entry for 1 June 1826.
9. Galt to Moir, 1 Oct. 1826. See *Memoir*, p. xxxix. Unless otherwise specifically mentioned in the notes, all quotations from Galt's letters to Moir are from those printed in the *Memoir*.
10. This passage, quoted in several studies of Galt, has not always been accurately transcribed.
11. N.L.S. MS. 6522.

Chapter 7

1. These quotations are all from testimonials which Galt preserved, and later printed in the *Autobiography*.
2. *Lady Blessington's Conversations of Lord Byron*, ed. E. J. Lovell, p. 146.
3. Scottish Record Office. The full exchange of several letters between Galt and Dalhousie is in folder GD/45/226.
4. *The Diary of Benjamin Robert Haydon*, ed. W. B. Pope, 1960, vol. iii, pp. 657–9.
5. Lockhart to Galt. N.L.S. MS. Acc. 5313.
6. *The Letters and Private Papers of William Makepeace Thackery*, ed. G. N. Ray, 1945, vol. i, p. 187.

Chapter 8

1. *Literary Life*, p. 318.
2. *Two Note-Books of Thomas Carlyle*, ed. C. E. Norton, 1898, pp. 249–251.
3. *Henry Crabb Robinson on Books and Their Writers*, ed. E. J. Morley, vol. i. p. 406.
4. cf. R. A. Gettman, *A Victorian Publisher, A Study of the Bentley Papers*, 1960.
5. N.L.S. MS. Acc. 4949, f.163.
6. Galt's letter, which contains Tait's draft reply on one of its blank pages, is in N.L.S. MS. 3713, ff.50–1.

7. Galt to Tait, 27 Nov. 1832. N.L.S. MS. 3713, f.55 — 'I am sorry that you do not like the third part of the Howdie'.

Chapter 9

1. The draft of the agreement is in N.L.S. MS. 4038, f.272.
2. Elizabeth Galt to W. Blackwood. N.L.S. MS. 4038, f.279.
3. *Memoir*, p. cv.
4. N.L.S. MS. 4038, ff.311–12.
5. The list is reprinted in Appendix 3.
6. Galt to Lockhart. N.L.S. MS. 925, No. 51. [Aberdein, p. 187, mistakenly cites this as part of a letter of 15 Aug. 1835 to Lady Blessington.]
7. The manuscript of *Ringan Gilhaize*, apparently unnoticed since 1823, was identified by me among the Oliver and Boyd papers in 1969. It is now in N.L.S. Cataloguing in process.

Chapter 10

1. Galt to John Reynolds. N.L.S. MS. Acc. 3098, f.165.
2. N.L.S. MS. Acc. 3098, f.166. An autograph hunter has torn off the lower part of the letter, removing Galt's signature and the name of the recipient. The handwriting is Galt's and the letter clearly belongs to the Galt/Tait exchange.
3. Quoted (from an unpublished letter) by A. Grant. *Susan Ferrier of Edinburgh*, Denver, 1957, p. 114.
4. R. R. Madden, *op. cit.*, vol. iii, p. 239.
5. Galt to Tait, N.L.S. MS. Acc. 3098, f.167.
6. Same letter.
7. 'Ettle' had a special significance for Galt. At the time when his ambitions had apparently been fulfilled, it was the motto he chose for the armorial bearings on his coach in Quebec. *Literary Life*, p.361.
8. N.L.S. MS. 925, no. 52. [Aberdein, p. 187, misdates this letter as July.]
9. N.L.S. MS. 925, nos. 52 and 51.
10. Dr Tilloch's will extends to close on 4000 words in the Public Record Office copy. PROB. II/1697 833.
11. Galt to Tait. N.L.S. MS. 3713, ff.74–5.
12. Galt to Tait. University of Edinburgh MS. La II 589, no. 7.

Chapter 11

1. Galt to Lady Blessington. *The Blessington Papers, op. cit.*, p. 61.
2. Royal Literary Fund, London. Galt file. Galt seems to have been ill at the time and the delayed receipt (signed by Mrs Galt) is dated June 1839.
3. A clergyman, the Rev. Mr Gilmour, wrote an account of Galt's last days. Moir had the account but made no use of it. The manuscript, with other papers from the Moir family, is now N.L.S. MS. 6522.
   The minister first met Galt in August 1834 and called on him regularly thereafter. He found the author of *Ringan Gilhaize* 'eloquent' on civil and religious liberty but when pressed to declare 'a personal interest in

Christ' the old man 'was silent'. At the beginning of Galt's fatal illness, the Rev. Mr Gilmour offered him 'divine mercy'. Galt's only reply was that he was feeling better and 'intended to spend the summer at Ayr'. A few days later Mr Gilmour had persuaded himself that the now speechless and paralysed invalid had by signs accepted 'salvation', but other visitors affirmed 'he was merely amusing us for an obvious purpose' and there was an angry theological confrontation at the bedside. Mr Gilmour firmly wrote in his narrative that Galt [speechless, paralysed, moribund] 'repelled the insinuation with honest indignation, confessed himself a lost and hopeless sinner in the sight of God, professed his faith in Christ as the only, the appointed, the All-sufficient Saviour: declared his belief in the written word of God as at once the warrant and the rule of his faith; and expressed his entire dependance on the Holy Spirit to regenerate, to sanctify, and to save.'

It reads like one of the horror scenes from *The Entail*.

4. This extensive collection is now in the Canadian Public Archives, Ottawa. University of Edinburgh Microfilm M.668. Among other things it contains the Life of Paterson (which was unwanted successively by Constable, Tait and the Blackwoods) and a short novel, 'The Predestinated or A Cameronian Mind in the Eighteenth Century', a tale arising from Galt's continued detached but fascinated interest in Scottish calvinism; it was offered, without success, to the Blackwoods on 1 February 1837.

Bibliography

I. GALT'S WORKS

The fullest bibliography of Galt's works, listed by edition in chronological order, is H. Lumsden, 'The bibliography of John Galt', *Records of Glasgow Bibliographical Society*, 1931. The present study considerably expands and amplifies the information in that article, establishing more precise dating for individual works and identifying additional contributions to periodicals. The specialist will use both works in conjunction; and a list of Galt's identified published writings of all kinds, with page-references to discussion in the text, will be found in the Index.

For most readers, the following short title list of Galt's main works published in book form will be adequate. Early editions, out of print but available in libraries, are included.

(a) *Published in Galt's lifetime*

Voyages and Travels, 1812.
Cursory Reflections on Political and Commercial Topics, 1812.
The Tragedies of Maddelen, Agamemnon, Lady Macbeth, Antonia and Clytemnestra, 1812.
The Life and Administration of Cardinal Wolsey, 1812.
Letters from the Levant, 1813.
The Life and Studies of Benjamin West, 1816.
The Majolo, A Tale, 2 vols., 1816.
The Appeal; A Tragedy in Three Acts, 1818.
Glenfell, An Edinburgh Tale, 1820.
The Life, Studies, and Works of Benjamin West (Part II), 1820.
The Earthquake, A Tale, 3 vols., 1820.
Annals of the Parish, 1821.
The Ayrshire Legatees, 1821.
Sir Andrew Wylie, 3 vols., 1822.
The Provost, 1822.
The Steam-Boat, 1822.
The Entail, 3 vols., 1822. ('1823' on title-page)
The Gathering of the West, 1823.
Ringan Gilhaize or The Covenanters, 3 vols., 1823.
The Spaewife, 3 vols., 1823.
The Bachelor's Wife, A Selection of Curious and Interesting Extracts, 1824.

158   JOHN GALT

Rothelan A Romance of the English Histories, 3 vols., 1824.
The Omen, 1826. ('1825' on title-page)
The Last of the Lairds, 1826.
Lawrie Todd or The Settlers in the Woods, 3 vols., 1830.
Southennan, 3 vols., 1830.
The Life of Lord Byron, 1830.
Bogle Corbet or the Emigrants, 3 vols., 1831.
The Lives of the Players, 2 vols., 1831.
Stanley Buxton or The Schoolfellows, 3 vols., 1832.
The Member, 1832.
The Radical, 1832.
The Stolen Child, 1833.
Eben Erskine or The Traveller, 3 vols., 1833.
The Ouranoulogos or The Celestial Volume, 1833 (illustrated by John Martin).
Poems, 1833.
Stories of the Study, 3 vols., 1833.
Autobiography, 2 vols., 1833.
Literary Life and Miscellanies, 3 vols., 1834.
Efforts by an Invalid, 1835 (poems).
A Contribution to the Greenock Calamity Fund, 1835 (poems).
The Demon of Destiny and Other Poems, 1839.

(b) Later editions

For full details (to 1930) consult Lumsden. The following single works were reprinted one or more times in the nineteenth century: *Wolsey*; *Annals*; *Ayrshire Legatees*; *Sir Andrew Wylie*; *The Provost*; *The Steam-Boat*; *Lawrie Todd*; *Autobiography*; *Ringan Gilhaize*.
    The major nineteenth-century edition of Galt appeared in Blackwood's Standard Novels, edited, with considerable 'illustrations', by D. M. Moir, four volumes being published 1841–3, containing: I. *Annals*; *Ayrshire Legatees*, II. *Provost*; *Steam-Boat*; *The Omen*, III. *Sir Andrew Wylie*, IV. *The Entail*. There were several later reprints from the plates of 1841–1843 and, as there are no dates on title pages, the binding is the only clue to date. If the books have been rebound for library use, they are virtually impossible to date. For bibliographical details, see M. Sadleir, *Nineteenth Century Fiction*, 1951, Vol. II, pp. 124–5. What was important was that Galt remained in print.
    Later editions of importance are:
        The Works of John Galt, ed. D. S. Meldrum, 8 vols., 1895. This edition contains the same titles as the Blackwood Standard Novels.
        Annals of the Parish and *The Ayrshire Legatees*, with an introduction by Alfred Ainger, 1895.
        Annals of the Parish, ed. G. S. Gordon, 1908.
        Annals of the Parish, with introductions by G. B. Macdonald, 1910 (and reprints).

Annals of the Parish, illustrated in colour by H. W. Kerr, 1910 (and reprints).
The Provost, illustrated in colour by John M. Aitken, 1913.
The Entail, ed. J. Ayscough, 1913.
The Howdie and Other Tales, ed. W. Roughead, 1923.
A Rich Man and Other Stories, ed. W. Roughead, 1925.
The Works of John Galt, 10 vols, ed. D. S. Meldrum and W. Roughead, 1936. (The 1895 edition, re-edited, with the addition of *Ringan Gilhaize*.)
Annals of the Parish, ed. James Kinsley, 1967.
The Entail, ed. Ian A. Gordon, 1970.
The Provost, ed. Ian A. Gordon, 1972.

2. CONTEMPORARY SOURCES

(a) *Letters (manuscripts, except where otherwise noted)*

Blackwood to Galt: Letter-books of William Blackwood and Sons, 45 George Street, Edinburgh.
Galt to Blackwood: National Library of Scotland (N.L.S.). Catalogued in N.L.S., *Catalogue of Manuscripts since 1925*, Vol. III, 1968.
Galt/J. G. Lockhart: N.L.S. and Bodleian Library, Oxford.
Galt to William Tait: N.L.S. and Edinburgh University Library.
Galt/Oliver and Boyd: N.L.S. Catalogue in process.
Galt/Park: reprinted by Galt in his *Autobiography*.
Galt/Constable: N.L.S.
Galt/Scott: N.L.S. [The Centenary edition of Scott's letters in unreliable for Galt.]
Galt to Moir: reprinted, often in shortened form, in *Memoir*—see D. M. Moir, below. Some of the originals are in N.L.S.
Galt to Lady Blessington: reprinted in R. R. Madden, *Literary Life and Correspondence of the Countess of Blessington*, 1855; *Collection of Autograph Letters*, formed by Alfred Morrison; *The Blessington Papers*, privately printed, 1895.
The location of single letters cited (e.g. to Bentley, Sir David Wilkie, and other correspondents) is given in the notes.

(b) *Holograph manuscripts of writings by Galt*

Ringan Gilhaize: N.L.S. (from Oliver and Boyd's papers, deposited 1970 — catalogue in process).
The Howdie: N.L.S. (incomplete — part I only).
The Last of the Lairds: N.L.S. (extensively corrected by Moir).
Contributions to *Tait's Edinburgh Magazine*: N.L.S. and Edinburgh University Library have a group of (discrete) sheets.
Mansucript volume of poems: James Watt Library, Greenock.

A collection of unpublished poems, sketches etc., taken by Mrs Galt to Canada in 1839 is now in the Canadian Public Archives, Ottawa. Microfilm in Edinburgh University Library.

(c) *Other manuscripts*

Dalhousie papers: Scottish Record Office.
Colonial Office papers: Public Record Office.
Last will and testament, Dr A. Tilloch: Public Record Office.
Pigott MSS: Bodleian Library, Oxford.
Minute Books: Irvine Burgh Council.

(d) *Printed accounts of Galt by contemporaries*

The following, which range from considered essays and biographies to short notes, contain information based on the writers' personal knowledge of Galt:

Blessington: *Lady Blessington's Conversations of Lord Byron*, ed. E. J. Lovell, Princeton, 1969.

Carlyle: *Two Note Books of Thomas Carlyle*, ed. C. E. Norton, New York, 1898.

Gentleman's Magazine: 'John Galt, Esq.'. (Obituary) July 1839.

R. P. Gillies, *Memoirs of a Literary Veteran*, Vol. III, 1851.

Haydon: *The Diary of Benjamin Robert Haydon*, ed. W. B. Pope, Cambridge, Mass., 1960–3.

James Hogg: 'Reminiscences of some of his contemporaries' in *Poetical Works*, Vol. V., 1838–40.

Frances Jeffrey, 'Secondary Scottish novels', *Edinburgh Review*, October 1823.

William Jerdan, *Men I have Known*, 1866.

R. MacNish, *The Modern Pythogorean*, 1838. (The introduction contains letters from Moir concerning Galt.)

W. Maginn, 'John Galt, Esq.', *Fraser's Magazine*, December 1830 (with line drawing by Maclise).

D. M. Moir: 'Literary Life of John Galt, Esq.', *Edinburgh Literary Gazette*, May 1829.

'Mr Galt and the Canada Company', *Edinburgh Literary Gazette*, June, 1829.

Biographical Memoir of the Author [cited as *Memoir*] prefaced to 1841 edition of *Annals* and *Ayrshire Legatees*.

Robinson: *Henry Crabb Robinson on Books and their Writers*, ed. E. J. Morley, 1938.

Sir Walter Scott: *Journal*, 1950.

W. M. Thackeray: *The Letters and Private Papers of Willian Makepeace Thackeray*, ed. G. N. Ray, 1945.

Katherine Thomson, *Recollections of Literary Characters and Celebrated Places*, 1854.

(e)   Contemporary reviews and criticism

The sources and dates, for all reviews and published critical comments cited, are given in the notes or in the text. The following contain significant information and commentary:

Inverness Courier, 10 May 1821: review of *Annals* (by Mrs C. Johnstone).

Blackwood's Edinburgh Magazine, May 1821: review of *Annals* (by Henry MacKenzie).

Quarterly Review (London), April 1821: review of *Annals* (probably by W. Croker).

Literary Gazette (London), 22 June 1822: 'Mr Galt's novels' (probably by W. Jerdan).

Blackwood's Edinburgh Magazine, June 1822: Note on Galt, signed 'C.N.' (by Christopher North).

Edinburgh Review, October 1823: 'Secondary Scottish novels' (by F. Jeffrey).

Johnstone's Edinburgh Magazine, October 1833: 'Autobiography of Galt' (by Mrs C. Johnstone).

Tait's Edinburgh Magazine, November 1833: review of *Autobiography* (probably by Mrs C. Johnstone).

Monthly Magazine (London), January 1834: 'Genius of Galt'.

3.   LATER BIOGRAPHICAL AND CRITICAL BOOKS AND ARTICLES

J. W. Aberdein, *John Galt*, 1936.

A. J. Ashley, 'Coleridge on Galt', *Times Literary Supplement*, 25 September 1930.

J. Ayscough, 'The Entail: an appreciation', *Dublin Review*, July 1912 (reprinted in his *Levia Pondera*, 1913).

Introduction to the 1913 edition of *The Entail*.

G. S. Beasley, *The Letters of John Galt* (thesis), Texas Technological College, Lubbock, Texas, 1951. *Kentucky Microcards*, Series A, no. 16.

Blackwood's Edinburgh Magazine, 'The novels of John Galt', June 1896 (review of 1895 edition, by J. H. Millar).

B. A. Booth, 'A bibliography of John Galt', *Bulletin of Bibliography*, **16**, 1936.

'Galt's Lives of the Admirals', *Notes and Queries*, October 1938.

(editor) *The Gathering of the West*, Baltimore, 1939.

James Bridie, *The Scottish character as it was viewed by Scottish authors from Galt to Barrie*, Greenock Philosophical Society, 1937.

W. M. Brownlie, *John Galt, Social Historian*, Greenock Philosophical Society, 1952.

F. B. Cogswell, 'Scott-Byron', *Studies in Scottish Literature*, October 1963. [Notes from unpublished Galt MS. of reminiscences.]

'Summary of report on work done gathering material for a life of John Galt' (typescript), 1960. Copies in N.L.S. and Edinburgh University Library.

K. M. Costain, 'The prince and the provost', *Studies in Scottish Literature*, July 1968.

A critical study of John Galt — in press.

D. Craig, *Scottish Literature and the Scottish People 1680–1830*, 1961.

W. Croft Dickinson, *John Galt*, '*The Provost*' *and the Burgh*, Greenock Philosophical Society, 1954.

Sir George Douglas, *The Blackwood Group*, 1897.

Introduction to *Ringan Gilhaize*, edition of 1899.

Edinburgh Review: 'Recent Scottish novels', April 1876.

'The new Scottish novelists', July 1896.

F. Espinasse, 'John Galt', *Dictionary of National Biography*, 1908.

E. Frykman, *John Galt and Eighteenth Century Scottish Philosophy*, Greenock Philosophical Society, 1954.

John Galt's Scottish Stories 1820–1823, Uppsala, 1959.

R. A. Gettman, *A Victorian Publisher, A Study of the Bentley Papers*. 1960.

T. Gilray, 'John Galt', *Encyclopedia Britannica*, 1879.

G. S. Gordon, *The Lives of Authors*, 1950 (reprint of introduction to 1908 edition of *Annals*).

I. A. Gordon: Introduction to 1970 edition of *The Entail*.

R. K. Gordon, *John Galt*, Toronto, 1920.

T. W. Hamilton, *John Galt The Man, his Life and Work*, Greenock Philosophical Society, 1947.

L. B. Hall, 'Peripety in John Galt's *The Entail*', *Studies in Scottish Literature*, January 1968.

W. Hazlitt, 'Advertisement' to third edition of Galt's *Life of Welsey*, 1846.

W. E. Hougton, See under *Wellesley*.

M. Q. Innis, 'A Galt centenary', *Dalhousie Review*, **19**, 1940.

G. P. Insh, 'John Galt in America', *Glasgow Herald*, 18 June 1927.

I. Jack, *English Literature 1815–1832*, 1963.

J. Kinsley, Introduction to 1967 edition of the *Annals*.

G. Kitchin, *Edinburgh Essays in Scottish Literature* (ed. H. J. C. Grierson), 1933.

C. F. Klinck, 'John Galt's Canadian novels', *Ontario History*, 1957, pp. 187–94.

L. Leclaire, *Le roman régionaliste dans les Iles Britanniques*, Paris, 1954.

M. Lochhead, 'John Galt', *Blackwood's Magazine*, December 1968.

H. Lumsden, 'The bibliography of John Galt', *Records of Glasgow Bibliographical Society*, 1931.

F. H. Lyell, *A Study of the Novels of John Galt*, Princeton, 1942.

J. MacQueen, 'Scott and his Scottish contemporaries', *The Scotsman*, 14 August 1971.

J. H. Millar, *Literary History of Scotland*, 1903. See also under *Blackwood's Edinburgh Magazine*.

B. M. Murray, 'The authorship of some unidentified or disputed articles in *Blackwood's Magazine*', *Studies in Scottish literature*, April 1967.

G. H. Needler, *John Galt's Drama, A Brief Review*, Toronto, 1945.

M. Oliphant, *William Blackwood and His Sons*, 1897.

W. M. Parker, 'New Galt letters', *Times Literary Supplement*, 6 June 1942.

Susan Ferrier and John Galt, 1965.

V. S. Pritchett, *The Living Novel*, 1946.

W. Roughead, Introduction to *The Howdie and Other Tales*, 1923.

'The centenary of *The Entail*', *Juridical Review*, March 1923.

Introduction to *A Rich Man and Other Stories*, 1925.

'*The Last of the Lairds*, a centenary tribute', *Juridical Review*, December 1926.

C. E. Skain, 'Galt's America', *American Quarterly*, 8, 1956.

O. D. Skelton, *Life and Times of Sir Alexander Tilloch Galt*, Toronto, 1920.

A. L. Strout, *A Bibliography of Articles in Blackwood's Magazine 1817–1827*, Lubbock, Texas, 1959.

Wellesley Index to Victorian Periodicals (ed. W. E. Houghton), Toronto, 1966.

D. Young, *The Use of Scots for Prose*, Greenock Philosophical Society, 1949.

Index

The index is in two parts. Part I lists all the Galt works mentioned or discussed in the text. Part II is a general index.

PART I: GALT'S WORKS

PART II: GENERAL INDEX